Kitchen Table Talks with Dad

5 Simple Tools to Become a
Transformative Leader

Angela L. Swain, PhD

What ARE They Saying About
Kitchen Table Talks with Dad: 5 Simple Tools to
Become a Transformative Leader?

Thank you, Dr. Swain, for bringing such a thoughtful level of humanity to the workplace in your first book, Kitchen Table Talks with Dad. You captured the art and the science of engagement with people at all levels of a small business. Weaving together the poignant reflections of the kitchen conversations with Mr. Swain and topics such as Emotional Intelligence, helps all of us understand how to be more kind, considerate and selfless at work. You remind us that not only is this a moral imperative, but one that positively influences any company's strategic position.

~Lauri Alpern, PhD, Open Door Advisors, President

This book combines an engaging story with quality academic evidence. Dr. Swain is a consummate scholar-practitioner and makes us all proud.

~Julie Benesh, Independent Management Consultant and Department Chair of Business Psychology, The Chicago School of Professional Psychology

I run my own marketing agency and I prioritize the emotional health of my team as a collective, just as much as the print and digital campaigns we create for clients. This book has provided me with a blueprint on how to continue to foster emotionally intelligent teams who are committed to the long game. I especially recommend the M3C method, which is a great tool that champions self-awareness. Tons of timeless and actionable insights in this book! Highly recommended for company founders and business leaders!"

~J'Arnay Harris, Founder/CEO of Legacy Strategies

Kitchen Table Talks with Dad is full of effective methods for truly building self-awareness and strong teams for entrepreneurs and organizational leadership alike, but what really makes it so powerful is how these are woven into and illustrated practically through a believable narrative.   As a leader in a small, family-owned business, I know how crucial self-awareness as a leader and empathy with, and encouragement of, the individual members of your team is to the success of the organization. This is a highly readable and insightful book for any team leader committed to emotional intelligence, and thus the success, of their team.

~Marrey Picciotti, Vice President, Albax, Inc.

As a business owner and team leader, I have always believed that highly engaged and committed employees are the key to business success. This book is all about people and how to keep employees motivated by building a culture of high emotional intelligence (EI) which fosters high performance, productivity, innovation, and growth. Also, if you want to implement the Diversity, Equity and Inclusion (DEI) program, you will find the principles and action plans as excellent guidance. This book is full of valuable ideas and tools for small business owners and people managers.

~Tracy Wu, General Manager, U-Lead International, LLC

Dr. Swain addresses my fears as an up-and-coming leader, and her description of my "why" was transformative. It's like she read my mind. This book is a must read!

~Scott Riley, Founder of Be the Flow Movement and Social Media Influencer

From her kitchen conversations with her father-in-law, Angela provides an invaluable resource for the small business owner. In order to realize true business success an entrepreneur must fully engage their key stakeholders, employees, customers, vendors and partners. And the level of engagement is a direct result of the culture the entrepreneur creates. Make no mistake, every business has a culture, and the savvy entrepreneur grows and nurtures a healthy productive culture. If left to its own devices an organization's culture can easily spiral into dysfunction. Angela's framework, that leverages Emotional Intelligence will prove most helpful to any small business owner/entrepreneur.

~Jeff Veeser - Gordon Food Service, Learning & Organization Development Manager

As business owners and corporate leaders, we take for granted that our team members have the skills of courage and emotional intelligence; those individuals understand the "how" to build a culture that supports a leader's life, not just their job. Dr. Swain's careful attention to each individual's experience, through the voice of her father-in-law and her research, is what is critically needed in organizations right now. And it's our responsibility, as leaders, to learn for ourselves how to build emotional fluency, so we can demonstrate to others how it can be done, and stumble - and sometimes leap - forward together.

~Emily Drake, CEO, The Collective Academy

Nestled within the pages of Kitchen Table Talks, I saw myself. I learned new techniques to facilitate leadership in teams and identified next steps for continuous leadership improvement...for me and my team. As a supervisor of educators who searches for professional text to help leaders navigate the leadership waters, this book, with its details on emotional intelligence and employee voice, is a must read! The content is timeless and would benefit leaders at all stages of their leadership career.

~Cheryl D. Watkins, PhD, Education Consultant, Author of Releasing Her: Personal Essays Wrestling Peace from the Jaws of Alzheimer's (release date August 2021

Dr. Angela Swain has provided the essential tools for creating a workplace where both employers and employees will thrive and develop into the best versions of themselves. Her expertise in EI (emotional intelligence) is woven effortlessly into personal and engaging stories that provide a glimpse into her own leadership journey. Dr. Swain's writing style is both research-driven and practical, making it accessible to Fortune 500 companies as well as small businesses and organizations. Furthermore, with the shifting nature of the workplace during the global pandemic, leaders will need to reimagine how they engage and retain top talent. This book is a must-read for any leader that is yearning to transform their workplace into a high performing environment, full of committed and motivated individuals!

~Dr. Andrea Brown-Thirston, CEO/Founder, Optimal Learning Solutions and co-author of Understanding Teenage Girls: Culture, Identity, and Schooling

This is not your normal modern leadership book. 5 tools for becoming a transformative leader in business and life has so much more to offer than just 5 tools. Dr. Swain has beautifully blended the core elements of family, work, leadership, and humanness into a wonderfully immersive reading experience that has something to offer for everyone. Rich modern behavioral sciences are united with empathy and humility. If you want to become better in every facet of your life, read this book."

~Matt Sandel, Director of Design, Behavioral Neuroscientist, DX Learning Solutions

Dr. Swain masterfully uses the art of storytelling and her professional expertise to offer practical solutions for organizational development. Her captivating writing style is a unique blend of personal and professional experiences to promote deep reflection. This multipurpose text can be used to personally strengthen leadership skills or professionally guide teams through organizational improvement. Without a doubt, this book is a must read for novice and veteran leaders who are seeking continuous improvement.

~Dr. Femi Skanes, CEO, Leadership EDGE, LLC Educational Consulting, Author of Encourage for the School Leader's Soul (release date, fall 2021)

KITCHEN TABLE TALKS WITH DAD

Visit the author's website at angelalswain.com.
ISBN ebook: 978-0-9980253-3-9
ISBN print book: 978-0-9980253-4-6
Cover by Brittnany Bindrim of Black Dove Design. Used with permission

Dedication

This book is dedicated to my father-in-law, John Wesley Swain, Sr. The character "Dad" is based upon him. Thank you for asking me hard questions, holding space for me to dream and become authentically me and challenging my limiting beliefs. Thank you for being "My Socrates" and for every memory I'll cherish of us in the kitchen.

Table of Contents

KITCHEN TABLE TALKS WITH DAD

Preface

"I have a doctor's appointment," I told my friend for the umpteenth time. I figured she would assume it was for my juvenile rheumatoid arthritis and not ask about it. In reality, I was going to the doctor about my learning disability. At my prep school, it would be shocking for me to talk about my dyslexia, so I kept it a secret.

For almost as long as I can remember, I had this feeling that I didn't fit in. Maybe it was because I didn't grow up with a father. Maybe it was because I wasn't in the "cool kids" crowd. Maybe it was because I just felt different and misunderstood.

What I did have was the most amazing mother. She showered me with so much love. If not for her, I wouldn't be where I am today. My mom is still my biggest cheerleader. She fought for me to get my education, believed I could do anything, and made me believe in myself even when I didn't want to. Any time I needed confidence, I just borrowed it from her.

Even though I had that support at home, I chose to stay silent in virtually every situation. I didn't speak up for myself and allowed others to define me. Because of that, I found myself constantly searching to fill that empty spot. Then, while in graduate school I started to question why I was even doing any of it. I told my mom I thought I should focus on raising my kids. "I'm a stay-at-home mom now.

Why am I writing paper after paper with seemingly no end?" She said, "Just keep going in the direction God is leading you. It will all make sense in the end."

Back in high school, my mom asked my cousin to tutor me. He'd graduated from the same prep school, and he saw my frustration, but he couldn't help me either. I cried because I couldn't remember dates correctly. Nothing would come out of my brain. I couldn't think of the right words. For example, I would want to say the simple word "cup" and not be able to come up with it. I could tell you the functions of it. It had a handle, and you could drink out of it, but the word "cup" would not come to me. It was like a brainwave was cut and the transmission of the word could not be delivered.

Then, during dinner one Thursday night after dance class, my mom and I were watching The Cosby Show. Theo mentioned all the same symptoms that were happening to him, and I turned to my mom and said, "That's me!" Later she called Children's Memorial Hospital, now Lurie Children's Hospital. They conducted a battery of tests, and sure enough, it was dyslexia. That's what Theo had too. I will forever be grateful to that episode because finally somebody understood me and heard me. It was as if they were in my head as I was studying.

We were surprised to find out about my learning difference because I was already in my sophomore year of high school, but now it all made sense. In grammar school I would lose my spot during standardized tests. A teacher even told my mom that Black kids were incapable of learning. By the time they told my mom about the dyslexia, I had held on to years of shame with the conclusion, "They're right. I'm dumb."

I remember my mom asking my guidance counselor, Mrs. Joanne Kelly, why I had done well in 7th and 8th grade and not now. She asserted high school didn't have as much repetition. Classes were structured as lectures; that's why I began to fail Geometry, Latin, and History. In fact, the principal told my mom that there was no way I could've been accepted to such a prestigious school and have a learning disability. Problem was, I couldn't describe what was going on inside my head to even know how to ask for help. So I stayed silent, feeling inadequate and disempowered.

Luckily, I had a guidance counselor who was on my side. She agreed to sit with me and proctor my exams. My mother told the principal that dyslexia didn't mean that I couldn't learn. It just meant that I learned differently. Back then, they called it a "learning disability," but my mother never called it that. She was ahead of her time because it's only now that we call it a "learning difference" like she addressed it back then. She advocated for me to be able to stay in school and receive the doctor's recommended accommodations.

There were about eight guidance counselors in our school we were assigned to, and Mrs. Kelly turned out to be the best one I could have gotten. She was kind. She was generous. She was very easy to talk to and she never made me feel like a bother. She didn't treat me like a child.

I could see myself in her. I kept thinking, "When I grow up, I want to be like her. I want those attributes." My friends would say, "Oh, I can't talk to my counselor," and I would respond with, "Oh, my God, that's not my story. I love mine." Mrs. Kelly was warm, embracing and came from a place of non-judgment. Like many adolescents, I felt like I was the only one in the school with any problems, but I could let my guard down with Mrs. Kelly. To her, I belonged there.

What I learned is that I'm not dumb at all. None of us are. We all have amazing gifts in different areas. For me it was just learning how to manage my dyslexia. I don't use it as my excuse; I use it as my fuel. I have to organize my day a certain way. Today, dyslexia is not as stigmatized. It's now under the Americans with Disabilities Act (ADA) and it's common for kids to get extra time on their exams due to their learning differences. Back then, I had held on to so much shame that I was suicidal and because I was hiding it from my friends, I never got their support. I never even gave them the opportunity to be there for me. I think I missed more 8th period Algebra than anything else because I was sitting in Mrs. Kelly's office- my safe space- allowed to vent and cry.

After college, I wanted to reconnect with Mrs. Kelly and thank her. I wanted to tell her what a huge impact she'd made in my life. Thankfully, she was still working at my high school, and we made plans to have lunch at a nearby restaurant. I thanked her for her influence in my life and told her how much I appreciated her. She told me she didn't think she did a lot. And that's when I realized that, while she did think I was special, Mrs. Kelly was just being herself. She was the type of person who knew how to make you feel important and supported. She was someone who would get into the deep end of the pool with you knowing you couldn't swim and think nothing of it.

Mrs. Kelly is the reason I went into social work. Now I have 3 Master's degrees and a Ph.D. My interest in human development was largely because of her. My mom has said many times, "If only those people could see you now." I know I wouldn't be where I am without the support of either of these women. I'm so grateful for these two powerful women going to bat for me all those years. They risked rejection and opposition for helping me out in order to save and rescue me.

I couldn't believe it when my mom asked me a few years ago if I thought she was a good mom. I asked her if she was kidding because I've used her parenting model, largely, to raise my three sons. She is and will always remain my rock and encourager.

I remember in the 3rd grade I had such a hard time learning my multiplication tables. Upon reflection, it may have been due to my learning difference, but we didn't know about it back then. It was hard for me to do because it was done verbally, not visually. Every morning my mother would have me practice my multiplication tables. When I got frustrated, she would put me in front of the living room mirror and have me repeat, "My name is Angela Louise Marie Hilbring, and there is nothing I cannot do." I think she had me repeat it about twenty times or at least until she felt I believed it. There were definitely days that I rolled my eyes, especially when she made me do it at 4:00 am. Sometimes I would think, "Yeah. Okay. Whatever." But guess what? I ended up winning a contest for learning my multiplication tables first.

We navigated an unknown space together, Mrs. Kelly, my mom and me. After high school, my mom continued to help me navigate every new and unknown space as well. When I think of these women, I think of how much they spoke up in my defense. This is why it's so important to me now to help people in any position communicate better within their organization. Just like Mrs. Kelly and my mom made me feel safe to share what was on my mind and speak my truth, it's important that employees feel they have the same safe space to communicate with their supervisors.

Acknowledgements

I'd like to thank all those who have supported me on this journey. Special thank you to my husband, Jonathan, for countless hours of sharing his story with me, my mom and mother-in-law who are the character of "Mom" in their combined wisdom, my childhood friends, Tiffany Smith and Sonari Glinton, for watering the seeds to transpose my years of study and life experience into a book and for championing me along the way.

KITCHEN TABLE TALKS WITH DAD

Introduction

For many of us, we've been told through most of our lives that what we have to say is not that important. If we weren't outright told, we may have felt it in subtle ways that resulted in quieting our voice. Eventually it felt unsafe to voice our thoughts and we ended up squelching who we truly are. Some people stop speaking up all together.

When this shows up in business situations, communication may be stifled, and teams might have a harder time working together. Depending on if it is the manager or the employee, different problems can arise such as misunderstandings, resentment, and unaligned missions. If instead, everyone learned to have a higher level of emotional intelligence (EI) and employee voice (EV), employee engagement would increase through sharing thoughts and ideas. Interaction feels easier to navigate and small businesses realize greater productivity, employee satisfaction, loyalty, and time on the job.

The foundation for this book is my study of the relationship between managers' emotional intelligence, positive and negative affect, and employee voice. I looked at these variables through the lens of leader-member exchange theory. This theory provided key insights to effectively implement emotional intelligence and employee voice in organizations. When I wrote this book, I was thinking of current and future leaders who are considering their approach to leadership and what it means to be an effective leader, manager, or entrepreneur.

Inside, I'll be sharing how to improve EI in organizations and what steps you can use to create and maintain a high EI company culture. I'll also be sharing the methods and toolkits I've developed such as IMAGES, IMPACT and Momentum Mirror Moments for Change (M3C). When you understand and apply the concepts I share, you'll be a better manager, business owner, and person. You'll have employees that want to stay for the long term, are aligned with your company mission and work together better, towards common goals.

Chapter 1

Emotional Intelligence in Small Business Culture

"The most difficult thing is the decision to act, the rest is merely tenacity. The fears are paper tigers. You can do anything you decide to do. You can act to change and control your life; and the procedure, the process is its own reward."
~ Amelia Earhart

Was it worth the risk? What if it didn't work?

Mom was always his biggest cheerleader whenever he had his grand ideas, but would she be on board with this one?

Dad thought this would be the thing that changed their lives. He wanted to make sure his kids didn't grow up like he had. Was this the right decision? It would take every last penny he had saved up.

He couldn't think about it too much right now; he was rushing out the door again. It took all he could muster up every day to go to work. His last employee review was good, but he watched other people climb higher, leaving him behind. While being a decently paid pharmacist, he wanted more.

Was that even possible? Did people like him get more? He knew that he was at a dead end. The proverbial glass ceiling stared him in the eye again and he wasn't getting past it because this was as high as a Black man in Chicago could go in 1974. As he clutched his coffee mug and quickly grabbed his lunch from the refrigerator, he resolved to turn in that letter he wrote last night once he confirmed all the information he was going to gather. But would he?

That letter would end the job he studied so hard to get and plunge him into a world he didn't know much about – small business ownership.

It had been 17 days since he had passed the "For Sale" sign in one of the grocery stores windows, and he hadn't been able to shake the thought of buying it. It was a place he'd gone before for bread, pop, and gum, but now he was wondering if he could run the store. What if he bought it? Could he, do it? Could this be a better way to provide for his growing family?

There weren't any other Black-owned businesses on the South Side of Chicago at that time, but Dad knew he wanted to give his children opportunities he didn't have and break the generational curse of lack- of education, money, and resources. It was his dream to give them a private school education and a college education with no debt, and the pharmacy wasn't going to cut it; he was sure of it now.

But what would everyone say? He already thought he was crazy. Surely, they would think so too. Time would tell.

Mom had always been that consistent "corner woman" for Dad. They had married right after Dad graduated and while Mom was still in college. Dad put her through college until she finished. Because they soon had a newborn, Dad did whatever he needed to do to support them all, eventually moving to Chicago with just $200 in his pocket. But it was Mom who always had faith in Dad even when he didn't believe in himself. She saw the greatness within him and the drive that was instilled in him when he was just a child, seeing the other kids with fancy clothes. He began young as a self-starter, getting a scholarship to college.

A few days ago, Dad knew he needed to get more information in order to feel good about going to Mom with his idea. He was hopeful she would say what she always said, "Inch by inch, it's a cinch." He valued her insights, but if it was outside his reach to buy it, the building was in disrepair or it had other big issues, it wouldn't even be necessary to bring it up. So, he left the house that morning committed to find out more. He had a skip in his step as he thought about the days at the pharmacy coming closer to an end.

When lunch came, Dad took the slip of paper out of his pocket where he had written down the number on the sign of the grocery store. For a second, he hesitated as he wondered, "Who do you think you are?" but the vision of what he wanted for his wife and children could be on the other side of the phone line. So, he dialed and found out that the grocery store was owned by a family who was moving out of the country. It sounded like it was a well-managed company and many of the employees were expected to stay. The building needed some sprucing up but nothing major needed to be repaired. It sounded like a good investment.

Dad felt like the grocery store was a good start. He could take it the rest of the way. His eye was on the prize of the life he could give to his family. So, he took it to Mom, and when he expressed some of his doubts and fears, she said exactly what he expected her to say, "Inch by inch, it's a cinch."

Sixty-two days later, Dad and Mom stood at the door of their new grocery store. The store itself was dark as they decided to close it for a week while they got to know their new employees. Some had decided to stay and try things out. Others had moved on to new employment. But the most important thing was to meet everyone as a team and then individually.

Mom squeezed Dad's hand, kissed him on the cheek, whispering how much she believed in him and how he was changing the lives of future generations in their lineage and community. "You are strong in the Lord and in the power of His might," she said and left him there to return to the house where a neighbor was watching the baby.

There were 13 employees waiting for Dad in the back room as he walked in. "Lucky 13," he thought to himself with a grin. Hurriedly, he walked to the back room. He was eager to meet everyone and share his thoughts about how to make the grocery store even better. The smell of freshly brewed coffee greeted him before he walked through the door, and he could tell by the looks on the faces of the people standing there that some of them were excited and some of them were tentative. Who was this man who had bought the store? What did it mean for them? What kind of leader was he?

Even though his heart was beating quickly, Dad knew that he had to address everyone with confidence as the new owner. He chanted to himself, "Don't let nothing kill your confidence," over and over inside his head. There were issues that they needed to discuss today about what things would change or stay the same. The store had seen theft rise, competition had come in forcing them to lower the prices of some of their products and there were overstocked products that weren't selling well.

First, Dad wanted to set everyone's mind at ease about what kind of owner he would be. There would be no "because-I-said-so" type of leadership. Instead, it was his goal to make sure that everyone's voice was heard. He believed that everyone had something to contribute and because they knew the ins and outs of their jobs, he would need to rely on them to share their experience and knowledge to get him up to speed with the store. After all, he had been a pharmacist and pharmacy manager, not a grocery store owner. The only thing he knew was that he needed to leverage the talents of those who were already there and honestly communicate the new mission and his vision for the store.

He started by asking each person to introduce themselves, what position they worked, and how long they had been there. He also asked them to share one thing they loved about working at the store and one area where they felt there could be improvement. It was his goal to know each person by name and understand their job so that he could create an environment where every employee looked forward to coming to work.

The one thing that he had learned while being a pharmacist was that if you didn't feel like coming to work, it was much harder to keep going. If he had good people, he wanted to keep them.

Kitchen Table Talks:

That night at dinner, Dad talked to his most prized advisor, Mom, for advice on moving forward. He honestly believed that his wife was the only woman he should be seeking counsel from and that he was the only man that should be putting money in her pocket.

He told her that they seemed to have a good base, but of course, he knew everyone was putting their best foot forward right now. He felt the pressure of getting it together quickly and making it "just so" because all their eggs were in this basket, but he also wanted to avoid mistakes due to rushing things.

First, he told Mom that he needed to assess where things

were with the business as a whole because, "You don't have to do it all, but you do have to manage it all." Then he wanted to assess the areas for improvement and roll out an implementation plan with the help of the leaders and employees. He would also meet with every person in the organization.

This process would likely take several months, but he knew in order to do it right, it would take time. In a way, that made him feel frustrated because he wanted it to be completed like magic right now. But he wanted each and every employee to have the time for honest discussion and to be heard, no matter if it was positive or negative feedback. Just because they were saying they wanted to stay also didn't mean that they would. If they needed to be in a different position, he would move them, and if they weren't part of the mission, he would be swift to replace them.

Mom listened as Dad talked way past kitchen clean-up. She wasn't sure if he had even noticed that she had taken away his plate and replaced it with a warm cup of hot bedtime tea. He just kept chatting and she just kept listening, inserting a thoughtful question here and there. Their daughter, Tabitha, had already climbed down from her highchair and was playing with her toys on the floor.

Finally, Dad took a deep breath to pause and looked up for Mom's advice. She could see his weary eyes, so she said, "When you feel stuck and frustrated, pause to step back from it. Take a warm bath, drink some tea, go to bed, and wake up early the next morning. Tired eyes can't see the big picture." She knew it had been a long day.

• • • • • •

What is Emotional Intelligence (EI) in Small Business Culture?

Whether you started a business, bought a business, or are managing an organization, creating a highly emotionally intelligent culture can help propel your business to great success. Your first question may be what constitutes an emotionally intelligent culture. In order to understand that you have to first understand what EI is.

EI is defined as the capacity to be aware of, control, and express one's emotions, and to handle interpersonal relationships judiciously and empathetically. As you may imagine, having EI in managerial and non-managerial roles means that those people are operating with heightened awareness, the ability to express their emotions, and can handle relationships in a positive way.

An organizational culture that utilizes and upholds EI is a culture where managers and their direct reports work together well, express their opinions maturely, without fear of retaliation, and contribute to the company's overall mission.

Experts believe that one's EI is more important than intellectual intelligence in achieving success. Why is this? Because your ability to understand and manage various personalities and identify feelings is paramount to your organization's managerial success. EI is not just about emotions though. It's a form of social intelligence that involves your capacity to reason, recognize, understand and manage your emotions.

Why is Emotional Intelligence Important to Small Business Culture?

When you can effectively manage your emotions, it helps to improve communication within your organization. High levels of EI improves productivity in the workplace as well, but the benefits of a highly emotionally intelligent workplace are much more than just impacting the bottom line. Your employees will feel happier going to work, they work better as a team, they stay working for you longer, and they feel a sense of comradery with all levels of co-workers. Having an environment with high levels of EI is conducive to help employee expression as well. Many of us grow up feeling like we can't fully express our thoughts because we won't be accepted. Some of us have even experienced negative reactions in prior work or relationship situations which stifle our courage to speak up. This leads to a lifetime of feeling silenced and misunderstood.

EI allows us to understand the effects and causes of our emotions which means we can manage our emotions better. If we have high levels of EI, we can also improve our performance by turning a negative situation into positive and productive behaviors. Because of this, high EI has been associated with managers and employees being able to work better together.

Gone are the days when commands like, "Because I'm the boss," are deemed effective. With EI, we all can become people with a purpose rather than just people with a job. Those who report to us will become more invested in the company and when they know that they will be heard, they will speak up with their innovative and creative ideas.

Emotions fuel many of our decisions and reactions. While those reactions can be subconscious, they still run the show. When we interact with others, we learn information about them and can understand what guides their behavior. If you know someone well enough, you can then adjust your responses to them in the future.

EI competencies are viewed in multiple parts:

1. Having the ability to know how people around you are feeling
2. Using emotions to enhance and guide your own cognitive thinking
3. Understanding the emotions correctly
4. Having the ability to recognize and manage the feelings within you

People with low EI tend to have an inability to manage stress well. This is why managers who are able to help increase their team's EI are able to help those same people handle stress better.

How Do You Create a Small Business Culture that is Emotionally Intelligent?

If you inherit a culture, you have to deal with past hurts, distrust, and owning your predecessor's mistakes. One important thing to remember is that you must reassure the employees that things will change in a positive way. If you need to create your own culture, you must be purposeful in creating it so that everyone buys into that culture and feels like an important part of it. In either situation, if changes are to be made, you may be tasked with proving that the direction in which the company is going will benefit everyone in the company.

As a first step, you must assess where your company is right now:

- What is working well currently with the culture?
- How might the culture grow to be more inclusive of EI?
- How would you describe the culture as it is today?
- How would you describe the culture of the future?
- What roles and responsibilities do you assign to management?
- What roles and responsibilities do you assign to employees?
- What training is required to transform the culture?

Common Mistakes:

- Failure to gain senior level buy-in
- Poor communication plan
- Ineffective leadership
- Lack of accountability
- Missing the milestones
- Going too fast or too slow
- Not recognizing or celebrating wins or successes

Why does this matter now? With all the changes in the world economy, innovation and the need for team building within organizations, EI is important. In our world where voices are silenced, rights are revoked, and systematic dehumanization of others is the law of the land, we can use EI to inspire, motivate, and communicate with employees not solely on a personal level, but also one that speaks of diversity, equity, and justice.

Chapter 2

Creating Great EI Leaders

"The mediocre teacher tells. The good teacher explains. The superior teacher demonstrates. The great teacher inspires."
~ William Arthur Ward

"So, what you're really saying is that we have double the work for no extra pay," Jason said to his boss, Matt.

Matt thought about the conversation he'd had with Mr. Davis, the new owner yesterday. He seemed like a genuinely good guy, but it was evident that he wasn't an expert in the grocery store business. As the general manager, Matt felt like he was going to be teaching his new boss all the ropes and it didn't seem fair. Shouldn't he get a promotion or something for this?

The other thing was that Matt's people (yes, he thought of them as his) would not be happy about the idea of spreading the duties of those who decided to leave the company across those who decided to stay. Jason just confirmed that. How could Matt approach it in a way that they could see this as an opportunity? He couldn't afford to have any more people decide to leave, especially since he had already promised Mr. Davis that he would stay.

"In short, yes, but it will be temporary," said Matt to Jason,

"But you bring up a good point about the extra duties that you're inheriting. It's a great opportunity to hone new skills and who knows? Maybe you'll want that job that Mr. Davis is looking to fill, instead of staying on your own. What if we all approached this as a growth experience? Because the good news is that we are all still employed. My plan is to sit with each of you individually to create your own growth plan. This is your chance to rotate, change or find something you didn't even know you'd love to do."

"Okay, now I'd like to go around the table and hear what your feedback is about the current acquisition. I want you to be honest about how you're feeling, and I want to know any area where you feel uncertain or unclear. I know for each and every one of you, this has impacted you in different ways."

The following week, Matt met with each of his employees. Most of them had the same question about what was happening with their job and if things were changing for the better. A few wondered if they should get their resumes in order and start looking elsewhere, but Matt assured them that he was on their side and that change was good.

Chris, in particular, stood out. He had already asked last year if he could have more responsibility and move up in the organization. The problem was that he expressed interest, but his work didn't show he was competent. While he arrived on time to work every day, when additional responsibilities were given, Chris hadn't stepped up to complete them. His sense of urgency was non-existent in terms of the request to move up. Now he thought these extra duties were an indication he would get a promotion and raise.

Matt had to reiterate to Chris that the past wasn't on his side. Matt would love to see Chris achieve what he expressed he wanted – to get to a managerial position that created the results, but month after month, he performed at minimal output. That wasn't how someone who wanted to move up acted if he was going to be a great leader. You need to first excel at your current position before you can get to the next or think about added responsibility. This one was going to be hard. It wasn't equitable to give extra duties to the others and not to Chris, but Chris needed to step it up this time. How could he encourage Chris in this big opportunity for him?

Laura, on the other hand, was going to be a superstar with this new setup. She was constantly asking for more responsibilities when she had free time, her work was often impeccable, and she took the initiative to speak up and implement improvements to their processes. Matt never had to worry or wonder if she would finish what he gave her. She really seemed to love being here. When he met with Laura, she expressed her excitement in the opportunity that he had shared. She looked at it as a way to gain more skills, learn new things and maybe find activities that she'd love to continue. She told him she felt like this was a great time to "reinvent" herself and her role in the grocery store.

Kristin was head cashier and the only female cashier in

their small grocery store. She seemed to know everyone who frequented the store and greeted them by name, so being on the frontlines suited her. She always wore a smile and arrived at least 15 minutes early every day. Many times, she would recommend to customers new products they were trying out in the store and easily got the customers' opinions. She was someone people always expected to see, and she created a sense of family with the customers.

Sandy was completely silent. She didn't work directly under Matt in her accounting position, but they interacted enough that he wanted to have a conversation with her. She had always been less talkative than the others, but Matt felt like she was even more so detached this time.

Sandy was a single mom who had been working at the grocery store for the last two years. She did good work, she was conscientious and polite, but always reserved. When Matt would discuss anything, even just the weather, she didn't say much. He had to make sure that she was involved in team meetings, and he would specifically ask for her input. Sometimes she would say she didn't have anything to add.

Matt felt there was a really intelligent woman in there who probably had some great ideas but was too nervous to speak up. Over the course of the last two years, he'd been able to get her to talk casually about small things in the hopes she'd be comfortable volunteering her other thoughts too.

Matt realized over eight years of being in management that sometimes being a manager is a lot like being a parent. He had learned a lot from his four kids, like how to truly observe your kids, see their individual needs, and find resources for them. You have to understand what their personalities and temperaments are too. In business, it's helpful to get to know everyone's individual personalities and highlight the abilities of each person so that your team complements each other. That's why you have to spend time getting to know the strengths of each person on your team and where they need encouragement to improve.

He'd found that some employees are just more verbose and boisterous than others. Some always share their opinions, some get emotional at times and wear their emotions on their sleeve, and yet others are intimidated in group settings and won't always voice their opinions even if you ask. But as the leader of the meeting, it's important to make sure that no one dominates or talks over another. And it's also your role to make sure that the people who aren't speaking are called upon for their opinions. Recognize everyone and make them all feel included. Besides, their opinion is needed, and you want them to feel significant.

For instance, Joe was just an all-around nice person. He had good ideas but wasn't always interested in sharing and participating. If Matt wanted his opinion, he would have to call on him, otherwise he gave off the vibe of, "I'm just here because I have to be here."

One thing that Matt did every day on purpose was to ask

people about themselves, regardless of if they were his direct reports or not. Most of the employees would say that they enjoyed having him around, working for him, and some even said they wished they worked for him instead of their manager. Why? They felt that he cared. He paid attention to them and treated them like they were somebody. Before Matt ever asked anyone to do anything inside or outside of his department, he would first ask how their kids were doing, how their mom was doing because she had surgery, or whatever they last spoke about. He made it a point to remember their last conversation because people appreciate and respect that.

In the past, Matt had worked for managers that were just horrible. They treated him like a number. You were there only to do a job and those managers would just tell you what to do. If you didn't like it, you could find other employment. You ended up feeling completely replaceable. It's not that you're not replaceable; you just don't want to feel like you are. Sometimes those managers even lost their temper and yelled.

The people who worked for those managers had no loyalty and it didn't seem like those managers enjoyed their jobs. These were managers who would repeat the company mission, but they were just words with no meaning. No one was working with them as a team to accomplish a common goal. After these experiences, Matt knew he didn't want to act like that when he became a manager. This was exactly what Dad saw in Matt and knew that he could depend on him to help him manage the grocery store.

Kitchen Table Talks:

That night, when Dad shared his day with Mom over dinner, he told her about all the meetings with the management team and employees. He didn't want to be that type of owner who sat in a glass office and didn't know his people. He told Mom he felt confident that there were some really great leaders, some dedicated employees and also room for improvement. He also knew there were empty positions that needed to be filled, but for the most part, they didn't feel extremely urgent because he thought he could spread those responsibilities across the people he already had. He'd get there in time.

Mom cautioned Dad about spreading those responsibilities for too long. They didn't want to hire too fast, but they also didn't want a bunch of disgruntled, overworked employees. They could end up with even more positions to refill. She said, "Always keep your eyes on the prize." That prize was the legacy he wanted to leave for his children and the life he wanted to give his family, especially now that another baby was on the way.

Even though he didn't have it all figured out, Dad told Mom that he was extremely confident they had made the right decision in buying the grocery store. He was excited about the future, especially for his growing family. It wasn't his vision that his children would inherit the grocery store, but the future would decide for itself.

• • • • • •

What is a Great EI Leader?

In the words of Jim Rohn, "A good objective of leadership is to help those who are doing poorly to do well and to help those who are doing well to do even better."

What truly makes a great leader is the ability to highlight the skills of their direct reports. While some people may think that EI means showing emotions or that emotions have no place in a business setting, the emotions in EI that we are talking about are the emotions that create better communication, empathy, and transparency in organizations. If we have high levels of EI, we can communicate our individual feelings better and understand the emotions of our colleagues better too. We can adjust our reactions which can empower our teams to move forward and make more progress. In fact, if you're a manager who understands the benefits of EI, you'll do well to recruit employees into leadership positions who show EI as well as technical capability.

If you're a leader in your organization, you probably recognize that everyone is unique. That means that it's important to get to know your team on more than just a surface level. You probably also know how essential it is to pick the right people to surround yourself with to get the job done. Your ability to inspire people, foster trust throughout the organization, have great listening skills, encourage creativity, and have relationships with your team helps to increase their performance; knowing who they are increases your effectiveness.

Why is a Great EI Leader Important in Company Cultures?

There are genuine leaders who want to lead the "right way," but they don't always have the tools to do that. Most think it's about that bottom line and while it's true that changing an organization's culture will increase that, it's not just about money. When you create cultures where relationship management, through emotional intelligence, is being addressed, then you build morale, loyalty, engagement and productivity, which significantly increases your bottom line.

When management and employees have common goals, they improve performance and job satisfaction. Managers help to improve their relationships by listening well, creating trust, encouraging creativity, and setting time aside to create and nurture the relationship on an ongoing basis.

If you have a high level of EI, you can regulate your own emotions and can influence interactions with the people around you, creating healthier relationships. When you can identify, understand, and control your emotions, you will enhance the social function of emotions and create stronger bonds. You can also use EI to prevent negative interactions and avoid problems in your relationships. Those managers who work on maintaining high levels of EI are more effective in managing and understanding emotions, which, in turn, leads to more beneficial exchanges between the leader and the direct report.

As a manager, if you're in touch with both your emotions and the emotions of your direct reports, you are more likely to avoid negative situations and create positive outcomes. Being in tune with these emotions creates strong bonds which makes it easier for you to predict the behavior of your direct reports in future situations. If both of you are working towards higher EI, you can grow it to greater beneficial levels. From there, your direct reports will feel freer to express their views and contribute to the organization's decision-making process.

By understanding your emotions and the emotions of others, you can better navigate relationships and increase EI. EI also helps you to develop effective communication skills while upholding assertiveness. EI helps to control anger, anxieties, and other feelings that can cause emotional stress. A manager's ability to manage their emotions may positively influence the workplace by being more attentive to their direct reports.

The way you interact with others indicates your level of EI. If you have the ability to be empathetic and motivated, you are displaying EI and if you are a team player who can communicate with others using strong social skills and self-awareness, you are also displaying EI. By using these characteristics, you can create and manage healthier relationships within the walls of your organization.

You can use EI to differentiate between different feelings and how to deal with those feelings. Employees with a higher EI are better team players, appear more flexible, and adjust better while avoiding ostracism in your workplace. If you're a leader, you should give overall guidance to employees while coaching your employees to attain your organization's objectives. As a leader, it's important to ensure employees complete tasks according to their set goals. Your leadership entails inspiring employees, setting future goals, as well as setting pace and keeping track of projects. A leader needs knowledge via training and education, and you will excel if you show personal qualities that help you in social situations.

The way that you lead can also affect the level of EI that your staff exhibits as well. Being able to identify your team's emotions and putting an emphasis on their thoughts or preferences generally leads to a clear and better agreement between everyone. Open lines of communication help your team thrive in the workplace which encourages your direct reports to feel welcomed in expressing themselves.

Being an effective manager means having the right skills to approach people and interact with your employees. In the same vein, employees in an organization need the skills to interact well with each other too. Through EI, you can improve professionalism and enhance everyone's career growth. In addition, you can create a good relationship with the leader and other colleagues when you help create a working environment that is truly open and comfortable for everyone. Evaluating someone's EI can also be an indication of whether or not they will be a top performer in the workplace or if they will hold low ratings.

How Do You Arm Your Organization with Great EI

Leaders?

Studies have shown that the level of engagement in an organization is determined by employees' emotional states or feelings. That's reason enough for a great EI leader to use their own EI to inspire others and build bonds to work as a team. Most of the time, all people need is to feel that you care about them, even in the office. The reason EI has become increasingly important as a topic is because of the rampant changes, competition, technology, and need for institutional investors associated with businesses today.

In order to assess your effectiveness in EI, you must look at: self-awareness, self-management, relationship management, and social awareness. By implementing an activity as simple as manager-employee swap days, you can give both sides insights that they never would have realized. And it's not just the managers who should self-assess; the employees need to as well. Learning to listen keenly whether the language is verbal or nonverbal is important to this process. When you can develop these social skills, you are more charismatic and attractive to others. You also develop the ability to fend off the effects of negative emotions.

Don't worry if you don't consider your company culture as having high EI -- it can be created. Here are some questions that can encourage conversations between leaders and direct reports:

- How would you describe the current culture?
- What might enhance the culture?

- How would you describe the current leadership style?
- What is your wish list for the next generation's culture?
- What could you do to move the culture to be more emotionally intelligent?
- What might you be holding back on?
- What is your suggested first/last step in enhancing the culture?

A Great Leader's Why

Many people say that they want to make an impact. In other words, they want to make a difference in their home, with their children, and their professional and personal lives. They want to contribute significantly to the world in some way, but they don't know how.

Sometimes we don't feel like we can make the impact that we're called to make because of the role we currently play in the world. When we change ourselves (we'll discuss IMAGES in the next chapter), we change the world and as we change, we remove blocks that are internal, external or perceived and this will allow us to show up more fully. Let's unpack this toolkit with the acronym, IMPACT, and learn why understanding this is important for small business owners.

Influence - How Influential Employees Can Positively Affect Your Company

What is influence?

Influence is the ability of an individual to transform and shape the opinions of others. Influencing the workplace, then, is a process of changing the behaviors of employees. For example, a manager can influence direct reports through their communication, policies, and actions. Influencing is one of the soft critical skills required for every individual, regardless of their position in the workplace.

Why is influence valuable to employers?

Being influential can be valuable. People often seek the opinion of influential people and listen to them. Your words have power. Those around you believe what you say and give weight to your input.

No matter who you are, where you work, or your professional goals, achieving more influence in the workplace is critical for success. Gaining power in a team can help you work together more effectively. Gaining influence in a supervisory position can make you more respected and appreciated and gaining influence in a meeting can make your voice more likely to be heard and acknowledged.

How can employers identify influential potential and current employees?

Influential employees can be your point people for championing culture change. These employees often help leaders get more buy-in at the primary level. They can be your eyes and ears on the ground, taking the company's temperature through the conversations they have with other employees. How can an employer identify influential employees in the workplace?

From their existing staff, employers can pick out the usual suspects first. These refer to the employees who are usually vocal and grab the attention of their co-workers for the better. Chances are you're already aware of some of your employee influencers. There can be overlap between engaged employees and the people driving conversations in your company. The employees that come to mind will be those that are naturally social with their colleagues, understand the business' marketplace and organizational structure, actively engage in company communications, and make an effort to connect with employees outside of work.

Aside from reviewing roles on their resume, employers can observe the individual's presence before and during the interview when considering if a potential recruit will be influential in the workplace. Do they command attention positively? This will help ascertain whether this person will drive change in the company if hired.

Employers can also allow influencers to self-identify. To avoid inadvertently making your employees feel burdened by bestowing the mantle of "influencer" onto them, it may be best to allow them to come to you. Put out a call across multiple communications channels letting employees know you're looking for go-getters willing to play a part in your communications initiative.

You may get more responses if you make it clear upfront that the role is essential and put them "in the know" before their peers, but it does not require a significant increase in professional responsibilities. As you communicate with your respondents, ask them what they're passionate about in the company. If you use them as influencers, identifying their interests ahead of time will aid buy-in and make for more engaging conversations with other employees.

Look for specific traits such as:

Trust. To identify an influential employee, it is good to look for the one that most staff trust. This does not have to be a manager or team lead. Influence is most often and most easily carried through trust. Only when a co-worker trusts you will they be open to your influence. If you're in a higher position in the company hierarchy, it's possible to convey a demand or assign a task that your employee must carry out. Still, actual influence suggests a free will component.

Assertiveness. Influential employees and potential new hires are assertive but not aggressive. Being assertive is the only way to get your ideas noticed, especially when you're competing with others for visibility, such as in a meeting. However, there's a difference between being assertive and being aggressive. For example, in an interview, the candidate will present their thoughts and ideas with a high degree of confidence, indicating their opinions. Still, any excessive degree of confidence could be mistaken for needless arrogance, which will compromise their authority.

Regardless of whether they are interacting with employees above, below, or at the same level, and irrespective of the discussion style, assertiveness should be a general attribute in all of their exchanges. Being assertive helps the influential employee build a reputation of authority and gain the power to influence their colleagues and staff.

Influence is an extraordinary asset in the professional world that often manifests as assertiveness and not aggression. The goal should be to become more respected in the workplace. One is a respectable journey to greater prominence and productivity, while the other is simply an unscrupulous power trip.

Money - Understanding the Value of Money and Compensation to An Employee

Money is a powerful motivator for many people. The wage a worker receives from his employer may have a significant impact on his organizational productivity. A worker's salary is more than just a number; it represents the importance that his employer puts on him as a worker. His degree of gratitude can have a significant effect on his overall results.

What is money?

There is no single definition of money. However, if an employee knows their worth to the organization they work for, they often consider their value in terms of the salary commensurate with their attributes and experiences.

Why is understanding money valuable to employers?

Understanding the value of money is fundamentally based on the focus of the value or the employee's self-value. While money is not always the central point for employees, recognizing an employee's monetary value can promote management's high regard. Money does play a valuable role in engaging employees. When an employee believes their company displays high levels of distributive justice (the distribution of pay, benefits, and resources), a workforce has a more substantial organizational commitment, has more positive job satisfaction, and promotes a higher sense of well-being.

There are typically three reasons people work. The first reason is to make money to support a lifestyle, including but not limited to paying bills, buying food, supporting families, and ensuring a viable future. Becoming contributing members of a society is the second reason; after all, it feels good to work and build a community and be a part of something greater than ourselves. The third reason people are employed is to be a part of something that can be accomplished, working alongside others as part of a social group and belonging.

Recognizing that the main drive is often money, employers must fairly address company-wide compensation policies and practices with as much transparency as possible. This will help equip the workforce to recognize their value but not feel slighted by the pay given to a co-worker.

When a company doesn't pay its employees well, the general office morale is low. Many workers may need to get a second job to make ends meet, which leaves them tired, overworked and resentful. Performance rates are typically low, as workers feel little motivation to exceed standards and absentee rates tend to be high. Employee turnover in these companies is often very high, as people don't want to work for a company paying below industry standards.

How can employers identify the value of money in employees?

An employer's ability to identify drive in an employee often brings them back to the monetary amount. Even though, as an employer, the employee's value should be considered based on the amount of money paid or salary and benefit given, many employees are driven by money and materialism. However, understanding and identifying those employees who recognize their value and are forthright regarding what they feel they should be compensated proves a strong-minded and honest worker.

Many employers find that culture and values matter most to their employees. These often are the most significant predictors of employee satisfaction and self-identification, which leads to recognition of the monetary value of their work. The employer who can identify such attributes in their employees can identify those who are potential leaders.

A well-paid employee feels valued by his organization;

however, an employee who doesn't feel like his organization is paying him a high enough salary is much more likely to look for and accept a higher paying position at another company. Therefore, employers can identify the value of money to an employee by observing their commitment to the organization and engagement at work.

A worker is more likely to perform to his potential if he's happy with his salary. A person earning a high wage feels motivated to do an excellent job because he wants to please his employer to retain his position. His salary brings him a feeling of security, allows him to feel accomplished and gives him a high ranking that he enjoys. A person is much more willing to put in extra hours at the office if he feels his financial reward, is a fair trade-off.

Keeping a motivated workforce is key to the success of any business owner but figuring out how to do that is not always as easy as it seems at first glance. Good wages aren't the only reason employees find satisfaction in their jobs, but they typically rank high on the list. Competitive pay generally makes employees feel valued and gives them less reason to look elsewhere for work.

Positioning - The Relevance of Positioning in the Workplace

What is positioning?

Positioning includes those duties and responsibilities that are considered part of a job description. A position is a form of power being held by someone in a particular area or department.

An evaluation of your current employees and their responsibilities is a crucial step in dividing duties. Eliminating redundancy in the responsibilities each person performs makes more efficient use of time and money. Assigning roles helps to distribute responsibility among team members and ensures accountability for all functions within an organization. In positioning, employees also can cross-train and develop new skills that can be mutually beneficial to them and the organization.

Why is positioning valuable to employers?

Employees are happy with diverse job duties; however, it is vital to have positions defined specifically to their responsibility. One of the most common sources of conflict and dissatisfaction in teams stems from the lack of role clarity between team members and between the team and the leader.

A well-defined job makes it easier to recruit candidates with the right skills engaged in their work. It provides a stronger sense of employees understanding their responsibilities. Providing positioning and explaining it well to the workforce allows everyone to understand their specific job duties and the overlaps of any duties. Discussion on such dual or combined responsibilities between employees can alleviate any issues that might occur, such as arguments over whose job is responsible for what work. A spirit of co-ownership is good, often more in theory than in practice.

Positioning is also valuable to an employer as it helps with more than defining job duties and responsibilities. Positioning assists with job bundling. Job bundling is more than combining two completely different jobs with similar responsibilities but require different skill sets. The positioning of jobs that can be completed through bundling prompts collaborative and detail-oriented focus from the worker; therefore, the employer's understanding of the value of positioning and the employee's value to handle such positioning is considered necessary.

How can employers determine employees' positioning flexibility?

Employers can identify those potential employees able to handle such multifaceted positioning by examining the employee's abilities. Some workers cannot multitask, but those can potentially have job bundling and multiple positioning within the company. The various duties and responsibilities that require an employee to handle several different responsibilities prompt a structured positioning. This makes assigning work to a given position possible as it is expected to be performed.

Once an employee is identified, the employer must also determine what the direct report is responsible for doing, how the jobs are completed, and how it relates to other positions. The employer also must identify all positioning descriptions because the description of such affects an employee's position in a multitude of areas, including assignment of duties, classification of the position, identification of training and development needs, recruitment and exam development, organization and planning of the work unit, and the establishment of performance evaluation goals and standards. Employers must identify and ensure their workforce's position descriptions are accurate, comprehensive descriptions of the assigned duties.

These employees are fearless decision-makers and natural leaders who step up when it's necessary. They are not afraid to make a mistake to reach for innovative solutions, as long as this is acceptable in the organization.

When asked to take on a new project, workers with a flexible mindset don't say things like "It's not my job" or "Do I have to?" On the other hand, flexible workers adapt their approach to tasks based on stakeholder needs and the particular demands of each case. Flexibility on the part of a worker could mean coming in early, staying late, or working on a non-working day to meet the organization's needs.

Employee positioning is also demonstrated by their willingness to learn and be coached. An employee may be able to multitask but is not interested in taking on new roles and responsibilities. Some employees may require more structure in their job duties than others who may function better working independently. Managers will often need to adjust schedules and delegate routine tasks to reach the company's priorities.

It is also true that employers must observe employees who

are self-motivated and can work on their initiative. This contributes to business success and continuity when challenges arise.

Alliances - How Strong Alliances Can Foster Growth and Development at Work

When it comes to facing daily challenges, having the capacity to reach out to a network of supportive individuals who can work to exchange ideas, find solutions, or stand by you in difficult times is invaluable. Historically, people have demonstrated the need for forming alliances. Strong alliances help to boost us and support us when we most require it.

What are alliances?

Most alliances follow a general definition of the association of two or more persons formed for mutual benefit or the relationship established between groups of people joining together to benefit a common purpose. An alliance would consist of an association of two or more people who all have an affinity in nature, qualities, and interests. Alliances can be considered the employment or employer-employee relationship as a mutually beneficial deal between independent players who have explicit terms.

In his book "The Alliance," author Chris Yeh focuses on "tours of duty" or rotational periods of employment. During a tour of duty, an employee commits to completing something for the employer. The employer commits to helping the employee advance their career, learn new skills and grow their network.

Why are alliances valuable to employers?

The alliance between employees and leaders in any organization constitutes the overall business's success, which is why partnerships are valuable. Building trust by making and keeping promises builds an alliance between employers and employees. An alliance provides confidence for both parties as the overall "mission" has conditions of success. The employee will benefit as they trust and believe the employer will honor this alliance. A positive work alliance is formed from effective communication, treating each other as equals, building trust, exhibiting total professionalism, and listening carefully and intuitively.

Information and support from workplace alliances are vital to satisfactory job performance. Your peers, boss, subordinates, and even co-workers who you do not get along with, can and should be in your network of allies. Strong and mutually beneficial alliances can help each party survive and thrive and get things done more quickly and smoothly than if they were to go it alone.

In an alliance, all stakeholders benefit equally. Each brings a set of assets that the other does not possess. It is an equal opportunity to create something that couldn't necessarily have been done alone. Employers who understand the importance of this mutually beneficial relationship aim to grow their company and employee by understanding each relationship's value.

How can employers identify an employee's strength of alliances?

Identifying alliances in the workforce is significantly difficult. There is no measurable metric that allows for such identification. However, an employer can determine other employees' traits to determine if alliances are substantially formed within the workforce. Observation is one necessary means for alliance identification. Watching how employees work together and address issues and problems as a team does reveal alliances.

Granted, this takes time, and viewing alliances may not be necessarily easily observable. Observing such traits as being supportive to others, nurturing co-workers, communicating effectively, not taking offense, and supporting those who are 'attacked' negatively within the workplace all are facets of alliances. Seeing team members assist one another with regular tasks, act loyal to one another, and give recognition and credit both publicly and privately are vital signs of employee alliances.

Some alliances develop organically. Team members may bond over a common purpose, target, or concern. For example, the senior colleague brings a wealth of expertise to the table, the team member who serves as a sounding board for your ideas, and the supplier who regularly meets deadlines.

Other actions to observe include being supportive, committed, willing to do extra, sharing the credit of a task well done, and building another's image. This trait in employees is also portrayed by providing moral support, appreciation for others, and understanding for those in pain or challenged in other areas of life. The cooperative employees are also those who forge the strongest alliances.

At work, allies assist one another in completing tasks more effectively and quickly. Having "someone in your corner" will improve your self-esteem, increase your resilience, and make your day more enjoyable. Allies can be found almost everywhere, both in and out of the workplace.

Creating and maintaining such links, however, requires continuous effort. Confidence and respect are the foundations of the best alliances, so you must be willing to support others and understand that they cannot constantly assist you.

Commitment - The Importance of Commitment in the Workplace

High levels of employee satisfaction in a company are linked to their dedication and involvement at work. This leads to improved business efficiency, which leads to increased profitability, productivity, employee satisfaction, and an overall better work environment.

What is commitment in the workplace?

Commitment is the bond employees experience with their organization. Employees committed to their organization generally feel a connection with their organization, feel that they fit in, and feel they understand the organization's goals. The added value of such employees is that they tend to be more determined in their work, show relatively high productivity and are more proactive in offering their support.

It is important to note that not all employees are committed, and they all certainly aren't at the same level of commitment.

Committed employees are an asset to an organization and add value in more ways than one. They are supportive and more productive than non-committed employees. These employees don't efficiently utilize their sick days and are more prone to adopting the vision of the organization if it's not already aligned with their value system.

Why is commitment valuable to employers?

There are several reasons why work commitment is essential. One of the most important reasons is it allows an organization to meet its goals and stick to its vision. Without a motivated workforce, an organization could lose all that it has earned over the years, be it respect or its market position.

Employee retention is a real problem. However, if organizations can make their employees feel valued, it leads to increased commitment at work, but without motivated and committed employees, an organization can be in a risky position.

Commitment at work leads to better productivity. Having employees who are not committed to what they do in an organization can be detrimental to the company's growth. Such employees tend to use their time to surf the internet for personal pleasure or even look for other job opportunities. This is a sheer waste of time and resources.

Committed employees bring added value to the organization, including their determination, proactive support, relatively high productivity, and an awareness of quality. Employees committed to work are also less likely to call in sick or leave the organization. Non-committed employees can work against the organization and hold back the organization's success.

How can employers can identify it in potential and current employees?

Committed workers may demonstrate their commitment by leading events outside of their desk-related responsibilities, such as organizing a volunteer project or initiating a lunch-hour concert. Commitment, on the other hand, does not always manifest itself in such simple ways. There are numerous ways for a dedicated employee to demonstrate how much they support the company, including:

> · Sharing job posts on their social media accounts
> · Referring friends or prior colleagues to new opportunities at your company

· Proudly wearing company gear
· Using company hashtags and core values in a positive way
· Consistently going the extra mile for their team and others
· Actively seeking out ways to improve their performance and acting on feedback.

As a leader, you won't have to wonder if an employee is committed since it will be apparent in their attitude and work output. These are the employees you would assign to a new hire on the first day or lead a meeting that a manager can't attend. They are the employees you can trust to get things done even in a rush. They usually wear numerous hats and tend to rack up company awards.

However, committed employees don't just happen. They are hired because of both company fit and talent/skills. They are kept because their growth is fostered by management. They feel appreciated and reciprocate with what they bring to the business daily.

It's costly to onboard a new employee but also costly to keep subpar employees. An employer can identify if a potential recruit will be committed by asking questions to ascertain the company's interest. They may indicate an interest in the goals and strategic plans for the future rather than just the salary they will be receiving.

Building a workforce of committed employees is a two-way street. As the employer, you must demonstrate prioritization of employee growth and acknowledge their successes. As an employee, go the extra mile. Show how your work contributes on a larger scale, and don't be afraid to share your great work.

Truth - The Importance of Truthfulness in the Workplace

We have no doubt heard the cliché, "honesty is the best policy." While this may sound mundane and basic, it is an important practice when it comes to business. Not only is honesty and truthfulness simply the best policy as a matter of principle, but it also makes good business sense. When you're truthful, your customers will respect you for it, and they'll keep coming back.

What is truthfulness?

The purpose of any business or organization is to make a profit. Therefore, for a company to profit, the employee and the employer need to be faithful and honest to one another and the customers. Truthfulness means saying what is true. To be truthful is to present the simple fact about something.

Truthfulness is a fundamental aspect of a business because it establishes the tone for the work culture you want to build, provides consistency in workplace behavior, and creates loyalty and trust in customers and prospects.

Why is truthfulness valuable to employers?

Valuing truthfulness and integrity in the workplace creates

an environment that encourages people to push the bar higher. Being truthful will establish trust between employees and employers. Being truthful about limitations allows team members to help each other and foster a positive work environment.

Employers value workers who avoid making false promises and stick to their word. They gain credibility by delivering what you knew you could.

Honesty is vital in most situations in the workplace. Being dishonest at work will usually set you up for failure.

How can employers identify truth potential and current employees?

Ethical people want to work for ethical companies. Truthful employees burn out quickly when they're faced with a career working with dishonest people, with no avenue to address those issues. A corporate or institutional policy of ignoring low-level dishonesty, or high-level unethical behavior, further intensifies that behavior.

Employees can identify truthful employees and potential recruits by asking open-ended questions. Asking open-ended questions will likely get you closer to the truth. The answers are usually indicative of whether a person is truthful in their speech.

A second way to identify honest employees is to keep an eye out for nonverbal cues. Nonverbal cues include forms of communication like body language, distance, and touch.

When some people are lying, they will "unconsciously try to disappear." They may also use barrier objects like a coffee cup or their phone to give themselves an unconscious zone. Other things to look out for include hand wringing, curling the toes and lowering or softening the voice.

Here are a few additional tips to identifying honest employees and potential recruits:

Keep their word: They establish a solid reputation by delivering on their promises without excuses and a change of conditions. Their yes is yes and where their convictions demand it, their no is no.

Keep their commitments: Truthful employees honor their commitments to themselves and others to create success. their ability to observe and keep their word impacts credibility, trustworthiness, and most importantly, peace of mind. They understand that breaking a commitment damages a professional relationship and their reputation.

Stay focused: It's easy to get tempted by distractions and other opportunities screaming for attention, but it's essential to stay focused on honesty and trustworthiness. Truthful employees remain concentrated on a job or project until they see the result they want.

They surround themselves with honest people: It is often said that birds of a feather flock together. Surrounding ourselves with people offering solid character and a positive attitude is crucial for a company's integrity as a whole. The people you employ should not only be highly respected in their field but offer significant influence on the others around them. An employee or potential recruit who surrounds themself with honest people allows integrity to permeate the air.

They take responsibility: Everyone makes mistakes, and this is true in both personal and professional life. Showing integrity means admitting to these mistakes and not being afraid to say, "I'm sorry, I got that wrong". Words can be powerful, especially when followed by decisive actions, so to be integral, employees must work to prove their remorse and be willing to take responsibility.

Honesty and dignity should have no exceptions in business. They should be practiced as a state of mind, not a circumstance. A company that does not value truthfulness will compromise their reputation in minor cases. This is unwise and can lead to greater repercussions and loss of trust from both employees and customers. Employees must also avoid compromising on honesty to maintain their good reputation.

Chapter 3
Creating Great Up and Coming Leaders

"I am convinced that nothing we do is more important than hiring and developing people. At the end of the day, you bet on people, not on strategies."
~ Lawrence Bossidy

Dad knew he had to put his thinking cap on and tie it tight. It was important to get some of these positions in the grocery store filled like Mom said three weeks ago. He couldn't depend on people and their good nature to continue to carry out duties that weren't originally theirs, but he wanted to make sure he was hiring the right people. Like the adage says, "Hire slow, fire fast."

In his past job as a pharmacist, they hadn't needed to interview too many people, except for the pharmacy tech position, but he had gone through enough of them to have learned a few things about people, in general. There were definitely skills you could teach people, but their demeanour, their initiative, their eagerness to learn, and their sense of urgency were personality traits that they needed to already possess before hiring into any position.

He had already gone through a stack of resumes and whittled it down to three for the position of shelf stocker.

The others seemed okay despite the interview nerves, but he didn't want to settle for "just okay." He wanted someone who could grow and would appreciate the current mentorship of the management team. Today, he was going to talk to the third candidate, Kim. She was working at a larger grocery store just outside of the city, and he was hopeful she was "the one" since the other two hadn't quite struck a chord with him.

As she entered his office, Dad saw a well-kept Black woman with upswept hair who confidently shook his hand. He began by asking her about herself and her background, then moved to questions specific to her role. He was looking for someone who could not only stock the shelves, but also work with Sandy who crunched the numbers about the hot sellers in the grocery store. He wanted to use that data to create front of the store displays and end caps so that those hot sellers were readily visible to every customer entering the store. The bottom line was to sell more products.

Kim shared what her daily responsibilities at her current grocery store employer were. She expressed that she was looking for a new position that would not be as far of a commute outside the city since she lived on the South Side, not too far away. She was happy for the opportunity to be closer to home and not spend so much time getting to work.

Dad asked, "What do you like the most about your job?"

Kim replied, "I would say that I love to see a finished shelf in order, lined up, where it's easy to find things. I like categorizing items so that their location in the store makes sense. Eye level items are the ones we make easy to find."

Then Dad asked, "What do you like the least about your job?"

It's here that Kim shared with Dad that, aside from the commute, the thing that she liked least about her job was that she often had multiple supervisors giving her instructions because the store was so big. From that, she said she learned to communicate between those supervisors better and clarify any time there was a conflict in instructions.

Dad went on to ask a list of questions. In all the interviews Dad liked to let the other person do the majority of the talking. Sometimes he even let there be three to five seconds of awkward silence just in case they wanted to share more after a thoughtful moment.

One of the things Dad was looking for in this position was someone who could communicate well and also talk to customers. The shelf stocker was also the one whom customers would see on the floor and ask for help with items or even opinions on which item they preferred. So Dad made sure to also give Kim some scenarios where she might interact with customers.

The next step in the interview process would be to have the candidates talk to Matt. Now, Dad knew it was backwards because in the future he would have Matt interview candidates first and then he would be the next interviewer. This time around, he wanted to be deeper in the process. Which one would he recommend?

Before he went home that night, Dad had a talk with Matt. He had come to really enjoy Matt's wisdom and willingness to provide his past experience. Even though the position of shelf stocker didn't seem extremely critical, Dad wanted to be surrounded by great potential leaders.

Matt expressed that one of the most important roles as a manager is one of motivator. Being in a smaller company like this, one of the things to remember is that there's not a lot of moving up and there aren't a lot of positions. How do you keep the people? You have to know through the interviewing process, the onboarding process, the training process and the development process that you'll be able to keep a person motivated in their position. A paycheck is not always the top motivator. In fact, he told Dad that there had been people who had come and gone with the previous owners for reasons other than pay. New hires would come in and take a pay cut if it helped them out and in Kim's situation, she might take the slightly lower offer because it saved on her commute.

Out of curiosity, Dad decided to also ask why so many employees told him that Matt was the manager they would most want to work for in the company. "Oh, that's easy," Matt said, "It's because I treat people with respect. You can try to demand performance and expectations to be met without yelling or treating people poorly. If you communicate clear expectations and they have a clear understanding, then it's a matter of just holding your people accountable after that."

Kitchen Table Talks:

On the way home, Dad thought about the three candidates he had talked to this past week. Maybe he should keep interviewing, or should he pick from these three? In interviews, most people, whether they can do the job or not, are going to overpromise their abilities. They put their best foot forward, so you have to use a bit of intuition in the process too.

That night at dinner, Dad told Mom about this last interview with Kim. He told her about the questions and scenarios he presented, along with Kim's answers. First and foremost, Dad had to determine which candidates had the ability to do the job. Then the additional part was the personality. Who will fit best within the team? Which candidate would complement the others' strengths and fill in on the weaker areas of the team? Are they a good match for the mission of the store? He also wanted to prepare for the future, not just next year.

Mom asked about the other candidates and how Dad felt about them. He recapped how Alex was the one that used big words to seemingly puff himself up. He seemed to have the job knowledge and the ability to do it. He was personable but there wasn't anything outstanding about him. Bailey was the other candidate who seemed knowledgeable again and could be a solid contributor, but there was something about the way she said yes to every question that made Dad feel uneasy.

Mom was always a great listener and continued to be attentive as Dad repeated how important it was for him to run a business with an inside and outside culture of being a great store. He wanted to show that a Black man could run a store like that in Chicago. There weren't widely known examples in America of this and he wanted to show that the store could have the same quality or better. Therefore, the service had to be top notch and the products had to be great. The store itself was a statement to the community beyond being a way for Dad to provide for the family.

Dad knew that he was apt to overthink things, wanting to avoid mistakes. In complete alignment with Mom's normal advice, she wisely asked him, "Have you talked to God about it? Don't overthink it. Just get it over with." She already knew who he was going to pick.

· · · · · ·

What Makes a Great Up and Coming Leader?

No matter what role you play in an organization, there are likely people who come to you for advice, to learn from you, or get guidance. In the context of this chapter, we refer to people in non-managerial roles as "up and coming leaders" in order to create a distinction. Up and coming leaders are an integral part of an organization's culture because they make up the majority of the small business culture. So if you want to create a high EI culture, you must first understand Employee Voice (EV) because that voice comes from the up and coming leaders.

Employee voice refers to the participation of your employees in influencing organizational decision-making. The concept of EV is about the upward-directed communication of ideas, information, or employee opinions that may contribute to a positive and collaborative work environment in your organization. When you use EV, it's seen as a self-initiated, proactive communication directed toward improvement which influences the decision-making process in your organization and helps it to be more effective.

Why Does Having Great Up and Coming Leaders Matter?

When EV exists in your organization, leaders become more aware of problems and opportunities to improve, or change based on the suggestions of the employees. By encouraging EV, your employees become more mission-based and feel more willing to communicate their thoughts, ideas, information, and opinions for constructive change to the status quo. This helps to improve overall productivity.

Often, labor-management conflicts can be due to a lack of communication, mutual understanding, and proactive resolution of friction. Therefore, when you have leaders who can encourage EV, harmony and cooperation happen within their team, even if there had been conflict in the past. In most cases, the sharing of ideas between employees and management is in two parts. In the first one, an employee speaks up and presents their idea to their leaders. Secondly, employees participate in the decision-making within their company. Because they are able to communicate their opinions, concerns, suggestions, and ideas to management effectively, productivity increases.

Looking into the future, the employees you have who feel confident expressing their voice are those who not only participate more, but also make great up and coming leaders. They influence your organization's performance. In addition, studies have shown a correlation between job satisfaction and EV, which improves performance, productivity and quality in your organization.

When EV is quieted, it becomes hard to improve working conditions as a whole and problems do not get solved in a timely manner. Frequently, employees are reprimanded for proactively seeking help or they are criticized and referred to as complainers. That's why having a leader who helps create an open environment for EV is so important. In that kind of environment, change can occur to improve the employment relationship.

How Do You Ensure You Have Great Up and Coming Leaders in Your Company Culture?

One of the greatest gifts you can give those on your team is to listen. Listening also involves recognizing where they are. Sometimes there's an assumption that if you're a leader, you know people because you see them every day, but they may be having a completely different experience than you think.

When you hear their story, listen because it's important to see where they are. They may say, "I slipped up," but it's important to put that story into context. What is going on in that person's life? What is going on from a macro perspective in the world or in the city? All these things have an influence on how people respond in situations.

Next, ask yourself what the employee feels or believes is a good strategy to address the problem? What does that look like? Even though we want employees to feel free to use their voice, that doesn't mean that every idea they come up with should be implemented. They need to understand that sometimes they don't have the whole picture and it's the responsibility of the leader to make a decision based on all the facts. It doesn't mean that you just listen to your employees to check the box of, "Yup, I listened," so you feel like a good boss. You do it to take into consideration their innovative ideas, but then filter it through the lens of knowing the aerial view of the issues.

Some employees get angry if you don't always implement their ideas and they feel like you're not listening. That's not necessarily the case. It's your responsibility as a great leader to create downward communication to say, "Yes, I listened and evaluated." You also have to convey that sometimes that employee doesn't have all the information that you might have to actually implement their idea. It might sound like a great proposal but it's a horrible concept to apply because they're missing critical information.

The heart of the matter is really about the mission of your organization. If you're focused on the mission, you can always bring it back to the mission. You take the emotions out of it and it doesn't feel like a personal attack if you don't go for an idea. It's good to note that focusing on the mission and getting buy-in are two different concepts. Sometimes workers hate their job but they can still adapt to the culture, which is different from the mission.

For example, if you don't have a passion to help marginalized teenagers, then you're probably not going to enjoy working at an organization whose mission is to help create better futures for those teens. It would end up being very hard to stick around. That's why having an effective hiring process can help you identify the right people for your team.

IMAGES

In addition to empowering employees to express their voice, another aspect to creating great leaders is understanding the inner work necessary to be great.

The framework of IMPACT (see Chapter 2), the outward facing concept that conveys "a great leader's why" is highly connected to the framework of IMAGES which is an inward facing concept. What do we have to do on the inside to make the impact that we want? This is what the framework of IMAGES is all about. It's about stepping into the fullness of who you really are -- living a full life, of being fully present and being fully engaged. In order to make the impact we want; we have to go within using IMAGES.

There is so much greatness in people and there is so much great work that we have ahead of us individually and collectively. It's important to take that time for reflection, because that is the way that we are able to show up 100% engaged in the world. When we take time to take our pulse, we can tap into that space to learn more of who we are and where we want to go.

IMAGES explores this fullness within the context of the workplace. How do employers know potential employees have "done the work" necessary to fully be engaged?

Intuition - Why It Matters in the Workplace

Often described as gut feeling, our intuition often impacts how we interact with people and who we choose to do business with, but it affects other aspects of the workplace.

What is Intuition?

Intuition is the "direct perception of truth or facts, independent of any reasoning process; it is an immediate apprehension or a keen and quick insight into something."

Intuition in the workplace allows you to know when something isn't right. A critical component of a business is understanding risk. When you incorporate intuition in your business process, you gain access to more profound wisdom and intelligence. Your decisions are more likely to align with your core values and a sense of purpose. You gain the energy you would otherwise lose when consciously trying to solve a problem. You gain greater access to creative solutions.

Why is intuition valuable to employers?

Over the years, employers have relied primarily on logic and empirical data to run their operations, and to their credit, many of these businesses have succeeded in their respect. However, most of the greatest companies to have ever existed have thrived not just on hard factual evidence, but with a combination of data, innovation, and intuition.

Employers value staff who also rely on intuition to aid their decision-making process. Using your intuition can help you make the right decision while allowing the necessary speed to match the importance of the decision. Along with fast-tracking your decision-making timetables, using your intuition can help you distinguish certain elements that logic overshadow. These elements are chiefly human and cannot be defined through complex numbers.

While aiding the decision-making process, intuition helps mitigate the effects of information overload, being overwhelmed in data and figures that you have no idea which way to turn—the task of cutting through the jungle of data before you can be pretty daunting. By the time you complete your decision, multiple other choices may already be sitting before you. This is where using your intuition comes in. Using your intuitive thoughts can help you expedite your business decision-making process leading to a happier workplace.

Intuition Fuels a Competitive Edge

Businesses must maintain a competitive edge to remain relevant and gain customers. Substantial companies can help to curb the competition by using intuition. As stated before, the industry is evolving. The only thing we can do is to develop alongside it. By using our intuition, we can gain a leg up on the competitors who may be change-averse.

Intuition is valuable to employers because it allows them to use every tool and gift available, not just physically but mentally, to succeed. As Albert Einstein stated, "The intuitive mind is a sacred gift, and the rational mind is a faithful servant."

How can employers identify intuition in potential and current employees?

Employers gain value from identifying employees who are instinctive. Someone with intuitive personality traits makes decisions based on intuition. Rather than formally analyzing a lot of information, the intuitive personality type goes with a gut reaction. High-achieving intuitive employees are often known for making the right call under pressure.

What are the characteristics of someone intuitive at work?
Here are a few attributes of intuitive employees that
employers can look out for:

- They tend to make decisions and judgments
  based on their feelings about a situation.
- They may not always be able to describe why
  they've come to a particular choice immediately.
- They're often observant and may be good at
  spotting patterns, reading people, and picking up
  on cues that subconsciously influence their
  decisions.
- They may be very good at making the right
  decision quickly, without much information,
  especially if they're high performing.
- Once they've made up their minds, they may grow
  frustrated by additional steps or hoops to jump
  through.

Workplaces are shifting from task-oriented environments
to requiring more complex problem-solving. The way that
business leaders made decisions in the past is no longer a
guide to making future decisions; adopting a multifaceted
approach beyond traditional reasoning alone is fast
becoming a crucial business practice. Such complexity
allows for creativity and a focus on the role of human
intuition in the workplace.

Given the changing landscape in business, it is necessary
then for employers to stop limiting themselves to rational
thinking and open up to the possibilities of intuition and gut

feeling. Frequently, that inner voice is powerful and helps direct decisions down a path of great success.

Mindset - Why Employers Value a Growth Mindset

Mindset is one of the most important factors influencing a person's personal or professional success. The things we consistently ponder have a direct impact on our behavior and actions. That is why it is essential to get a clear understanding of the idea of mindset.

Though it may seem trivial, our mindset makes a huge difference and accounts for the primary distinction between people who succeed and people who do not. Anyone determined to achieve success in any area of their life must learn to master their mindset.

What is Mindset?

Mindset, in simple terms, is a way of thinking. It is a mental inclination or disposition or a frame of mind. Your mindset is your collection of thoughts and beliefs that shape your thought habits. And your thought habits affect how you think, what you feel, and what you do. Your mindset impacts how you make sense of the world and how you perceive yourself.

It is often categorized into two types: a fixed mindset or a growth mindset. People with a fixed mindset believe their essential qualities, like their intelligence or talent, are fixed traits. They also believe that talent alone creates success—without effort. On the other hand, people with a growth mindset believe that their most basic abilities can be developed through dedication and hard work—brains and talent are just the starting point. This view creates a love of learning and resilience that is essential for great accomplishment.

Why is a growth mindset valuable to employers?

Our mindset plays a critical role in how we cope with life's challenges. A growth mindset can contribute to more outstanding achievement and increased effort. When facing a challenge, people with growth mindsets show greater resilience. They are more likely to persevere in the face of setbacks, while those with fixed mindsets are more likely to give up.

For employers, an optimistic demeanor shows that you have the confidence in your skill set to perform in your role. It demonstrates a "can do" attitude that is essential to the company's growth, especially when difficulties arise.

Employees and executives with growth mindsets are essential assets in companies because they see challenges as learning opportunities. They learn from their mistakes and use the experience to avoid repeating these in the future. Individuals with a growth mindset respect hard work and commitment, and they are more likely to resist distractions that might cause them to lose focus.

How can employers identify growth mindset in potential and current employees?

Individuals with a growth mindset believe that they can develop their talents. They aren't stuck with the skills and aptitudes they currently possess. When identifying this in potential and current employees, it is essential to look for employees who are willing to learn and use positive language.

For example, the language used in the application and interview of someone with an optimistic mindset is different from that of someone without one.

A person who demonstrates a growth mindset embraces challenges and persists in the face of setbacks. They view effort as a path to mastery and not as excessive work or pointless activity. These employees learn from criticism and find lessons and inspiration from the success of others.

In an interview setting, an employer can identify the mindset of an employee by presenting viewpoint questions that allow them to express their feelings. You may ask the employee to give an example of a mission or goal they didn't think was achievable initially and how they eventually overcame it. Allow the individual to express thoughts on things that help them bounce back from challenges and share their views on continuous learning.

Providing feedback to potential and existing employees and gauging their response to the input and their actions are ways to indicate a fixed mindset or a growth mindset.

Applying a growth mindset can transform a stagnant

workplace into a haven for innovation, but without it, employees, leaders, and the company may never reach their full potential. Extending beyond just your personal goals and aspirations, the decision between a fixed and growth mindset also has dramatic implications in your professional life. Whether a CEO or an entry-level salesman, carrying yourself with a growth mindset can help create a better environment for your team and lead toward success.

Awareness - The Importance of Self-Awareness in Employees

Self-awareness is the ability to monitor your own emotions and reactions. Self-awareness enables you to recognize your capabilities, limitations, causes, motivators, and other traits. Being self-aware entails taking a closer look at your feelings, why you feel the way you do, and how your emotions can manifest as reactions.

Why is awareness valuable to employers?

Employers value awareness because it also fosters an environment of growth and personal development. Once we understand ourselves, we begin to know how we are different from other people. When we know these differences, we start to appreciate how we can work more effectively with others.

It is essential to understand why people behave the way they do because it gives a greater understanding of our reactions and motivation, better management of oneself and others, the ability to adapt our behavior accordingly, and improved relationships and personal growth. Increased self-awareness is also beneficial when working with others in a team.

A high degree of self-awareness helps individuals understand and fully know their strengths, weaknesses, what motivates or demotivates them, and other vital aspects of their personality in every area of life.

Self-awareness in employees is even more relevant and vital simply because, at work, we are interacting with strangers and people who we are not close to, and it requires even more effort to relate to them positively. By encouraging self-awareness in employees, companies can ensure that they are more mindful of their behavior and consistently work on improving themselves. Self-awareness in employees helps them understand and appreciate their shortcomings and those of their co-workers and those they interact with daily, including customers.

This is valuable to employers because self-aware employees tend to be more in control emotionally and adjust their behavior with others. Each person can work in a stress-free and congenial work environment. The attainment of goals and vision is a lot easier when each person in the company works towards them together rather than against each other.

Self-awareness in employees helps each person to objectively judge situations and people's responses and remain aware that their co-workers would have different opinions that deserve respect. To create a healthy work environment, it would be helpful for companies to help their employees build and consistently strive towards self-awareness.

How can employers identify self-awareness in potential and current employees?

Employers will observe specific skills in employees who have a high level of self-awareness. They are:

Open-minded

Self-aware employees and potential new hires are usually open-minded. When you can regulate your emotional world, you can be attuned to others' emotions. To be a successful leader, you have to be curious about new people and all they have to offer. Self-aware employees are usually good team players and don't always see the need to be on top.

Mindful of their strengths and weaknesses

Self-aware individuals know their strengths and weaknesses and can work from that space. Being mindful of this means that they know when to reach out for assistance and when they can work on their own.

Focused

An essential part of being self-aware is making

connections, but this is harder to accomplish when distracted. Self-aware employees can focus for long periods without getting sucked into social media, emails, and other minor interruptions.

Set boundaries

Self-aware employees have firm boundaries in place. They are warm toward others but say no when they need to. They understand their limitations yet are serious about their work and passions. These employees keep their boundaries firm to maintain the integrity of their goals and the work they put into them.

Aware of their emotional triggers

Self-aware individuals can identify their emotions as they are happening. This doesn't mean they repress their feelings or deny the causes, but instead, they can bend and flex with them and fully process them before communicating with others. Of course, no one is perfect, but they are usually measured in their responses and do not overreact.

Practice self-discipline

Self-aware individuals tend to be disciplined in every area of their life. It is a character trait that provides them with the enduring focus necessary for strong leadership.

Employees with a high level of self-awareness feel more linked to the company's performance and are more likely to go above and beyond to help it reach new heights. Building employee self-awareness is one of the most powerful management techniques. Businesses must look for ways to improve it, whether with the assistance of experts or through readily accessible online tools.

Guidance Can Foster a Successful Work Environment

American author Brian Herbert once said, "The capacity to learn is a gift; the ability to learn is a skill; the willingness to learn is a choice." In the workplace, this statement reigns true and can be vital to the success of any company. Employees who are willing to learn or be guided, coupled with employers who invest in guidance and coaching, are a powerful combination for a successful business.

What is guidance in the workplace?

Guidance in the workplace can take on two aspects: coaching employees and the steps employees take to learn. Coaching refers to addressing performance objectives and helping direct reports perform optimally. According to Harvard Business Review, coaching provides an opportunity to act as a sounding board, facilitate transitions, and address derailing behavior. Rather than traditional performance management systems, coaching allows leaders to communicate immediate changes or actions to be taken by employees that can improve the performance of the individual, team, and organization.

On the part of an employee, a willingness to learn is the desire to gain knowledge and develop skills to improve their work performance. Employees who demonstrate a desire to learn always search for new opportunities to stay ahead of modern trends, achieve professional goals and complete more challenging tasks. Showing that you're willing to learn tells employers that you're a hardworking, driven and motivated team member. It is a desire, wish or readiness to acquire new knowledge and develop. It means that a person does not want to stand in one place for the duration of their career.

Why is guidance valuable to employers?

A willingness to learn is essential because it demonstrates to your employers that you are interested in learning new skills and abilities that may lead to promotions and possibly raises. Employers are often impressed with the drive and determination of an employee who wants to acquire new job responsibilities.

When complex and unexpected workplace problems arise, an employee who is willing to learn can work hard to overcome these challenges and grow from the experience. They understand which areas they excel at and where they can improve. This is important to employers.

Employers and employees who are also willing to coach and train others provide career assistance for junior employees and less experienced staff. This can prevent minor problems from getting out of hand and creating more significant barriers to success. It's also a way to help key employees reach higher career aspirations so that they continue to add considerable value to the company.

How can employers identify potential and current employees who are willing to learn and be coached?

Employees and potential recruits who are willing to learn and be guided will ask lots of questions. They do not do this to probe but instead to gain insight and knowledge of a task. A potential employee who uses the interview to ask questions about the company and the role allows hiring managers to gain as much information as possible about the position to ensure it's right for them. This also tells interviewers that they won't be hesitant to ask questions if they are having difficulties performing a workplace task or learning more about a particular skill or responsibility.

These employees demonstrate their passion for gaining new skills. If they have little to no work experience, expressing a willingness to learn new skills indicates to their manager that they are hardworking and passionate and interested in moving forward with their company.

When you're willing to learn, you typically have the self-motivation and determination to teach yourself and others new skills. A potential recruit will demonstrate their drive to learn by stating examples when they did a course or learned something new on their initiative.

Employees who are willing to be guided are always seeking to earn certifications and take additional courses. They request information about training and growth opportunities, and they pitch new ideas based on their research.

Whether in a leadership position or not, employers can also identify employees who are willing to coach and guide others by their attitudes towards new responsibilities and new staff. These employees often willingly volunteer for opportunities to train junior staff or present new ideas in meetings. Employers would do well to take note of these traits to promote and encourage them where possible.

Coaching in the workplace can help create stronger bonds within your team. As team members become more comfortable with leaders, they'll be more willing to seek help when problems arise. Building more intentional relationships with employees through coaching makes them feel included.

Emotional Intelligence

Emotional intelligence is an essential aspect of our professional lives. It gives us the ability to understand and manage our emotions effectively. This skill will help you advance your career and provide significant benefits in the workplace.

What is emotional intelligence?

Emotional intelligence is the capacity to understand and manage your emotions. The skills involved in emotional intelligence are self-awareness, self-regulation, motivation, empathy, and social skills. Embracing the distinctions of human emotion in the workplace can have practical benefits, such as better collabbration among employees and a happier workplace.

Why is emotional intelligence valuable to employers?

Emotional intelligence has become an essential topic in the workplace. It is valuable to employers because it means employees can perceive, reason with, understand and manage their emotions and others. Being able to handle emotions gives you the ability to guide and help people. Being emotionally intelligent also gives you the ability to understand non-verbal communication. Strong emotional intelligence will enable you to fix a situation before it becomes a problem.

Understanding emotions allows you to be self-aware of personal feelings. You can use this skill to adjust your behavior before it becomes an issue for a client or co-worker. Practicing emotional intelligence can help you develop strong interpersonal skills to help your team and inspire your whole company. Emotions are contagious, and displaying explicit motivation, empathy, responsibility, and teamwork could encourage your team to follow along.

Employers also value emotional intelligence because it promotes progress. When people are empathetic and understand each other's emotions, employees can make decisions with ease and complete tasks more efficiently.

How can employers identify emotional intelligence in potential and current employees?

Unlike intellectual capacity, emotional intelligence is less cut and dry. Employers must understand the skills required to be emotionally intelligent to identify them in potential and current employees.

Self-Aware: Emotionally intelligent employees are aware of their strengths and weaknesses. These employees can take feedback and use it positively to improve and grow as an individual. Even if the feedback they receive could be pretty revealing, they are willing to learn from it. While emotionally intelligent people know themselves and what they can accomplish in a set amount of time, others are more likely to overpromise and underdeliver. Employees with high emotional intelligence can learn from constructive criticism and be aware of what they can do.

Not afraid to Ask for help: To improve emotional intelligence in the workplace, asking for help can be a critical tool. Employees who think they can go it alone are usually not team players and may even take on more than they can manage. Emotionally intelligent employees are not afraid to ask for help and state when they may be facing challenges.

Demonstrates more self-control: People with high emotional intelligence know how to handle challenging situations. In business, there are bound to be situations that don't always feel comfortable, particularly for a person acting in a leadership position.

A challenging situation could involve an unhappy client. Dealing with unhappy clients means staying calm and positive, even if you don't necessarily feel that way on the inside. A tough situation could be a manager who is unhappy with your work. This creates a sense of unease and embarrassment. It could be a challenging conversation with a junior, either involving disciplinary action or firing. In situations like these, a person needs to be firm yet kind. This means holding an understanding mind and remaining calm. If an employee can refrain from an emotional outburst and stay calm in situations like these, it can be better.

More compassionate: One of the most incredible benefits of emotional intelligence, both within the workplace and in one's personal life, is the ability to maintain and display compassion for fellow humans. Empathy allows a person to connect with others on an emotional level.

This can be a great benefit to an employer when their workers display compassion. Compassion can be shared with a client that missed a payment due to a challenging circumstance.

Compassion can be shown to a co-worker dealing with a personal issue and needing someone to cover their responsibilities. Empathy can also be demonstrated to leadership for the decisions they need to make daily.

More motivated: Emotionally Intelligent individuals are optimistic and are always naturally working towards a goal, whether personal, professional or both. These individuals have a growth mindset, and they persevere no matter the obstacles they face.

These employees are often not motivated by external means but rather are driven by their inner ambition. People with high emotional intelligence work hard for the benefit of knowing they completed the job successfully.

Stress Management - Effective Stress Management in the Workplace

We all have experienced stress and feelings of anxiety at some point in our lives. Stress manifests itself in different ways and may cause us to become overwhelmed and frustrated. It is crucial to understand how to manage stress in our personal and professional lives. Stress management is an essential tool that employers must teach in the workplace and employees must learn to foster a better work environment.

What is stress management?

Stress management is a broad spectrum of techniques and psychotherapies aimed at controlling a person's level of stress, especially chronic stress, usually for the motive of improving everyday functioning.

Managing stress is all about taking charge: taking charge of your thoughts, your emotions, your schedule, your environment, and the way you deal with problems. The ultimate goal is a balanced life, with time for work, relationships, relaxation, and fun – plus the resilience to hold up under pressure and meet challenges head-on.

Why is stress management valuable to employers?

Employers do well to foster an environment that emphasizes stress management as a tool for professional development. It is vital to ensure a strong company culture: Healthier employees operating under manageable levels of stress will be happier and more positive, helping to maintain a robust and healthy workplace culture conducive to creativity and productivity.

Stress management also leads to less sick days and increased productivity. Stress is one of the leading causes of absenteeism in the workplace. Not only will less stress in the workplace result in fewer "mental health days," but it will also reduce the number of sick days taken by employees due to a weakened immune system resulting from excessive stress.

If you value employee retention and talent acquisition, then stress management will also be high on your list of activities for your employee. Employees who aren't overly stressed are much more likely to stick around and prospective employees are much more likely to work for an employer that promotes a low-stress work environment and takes the initiative to help keep their employees healthy.

How can employers identify potential and current employees who are managing stress effectively?

While there is no set way to identify an employee effectively managing their stress levels, there are some indicators that you can look for as an employer.

They have developed healthy responses.

Instead of fighting stress with fast food or addictions, these employees promote and practice a healthy lifestyle. Whether it is yoga or exercise, they take part in some healthy physical activity. They also make time for hobbies and other activities outside of work.

They establish boundaries.

In today's digital world, it's easy to feel pressure to be available 24 hours a day. While employers want the freedom to have employees on call, it is alarming if they are always available and do not set work-life boundaries. Potential hires who indicate that they are always available and do not highlight limitations may say what is necessary to get a job but may not be able to manage this if the situation arises.

Establishing boundaries might mean employers do not expect employees to be on call 24/7. Additionally, employees can make a rule not to check email from home in the evening or not to answer the phone during dinner. Although people have different preferences regarding how much they blend their work and home life, creating some clear boundaries between these realms can reduce the potential for work-life conflict and the stress that goes with it.

They take time to recharge.

To avoid the harmful effects of chronic stress and burnout, we need time to replenish and return to our pre-stress level of functioning. This recovery process requires "switching off" from work by having periods when we are neither engaging in work-related activities nor thinking about work. Dedication to a company is highly sought after and commendable, but employees who disconnect are often more productive and indicate effective stress management. They don't let vacation days go to waste and take the necessary time off to relax and unwind, so they come back to work feeling reinvigorated and ready to perform at their best.

They get support when necessary.

Employees and potential new hires who accept help from others in the workplace can improve their ability to manage stress. They are not afraid to utilize stress management resources available through an employee assistance program, including online information, general counseling, and referral to mental health professionals, if needed.

Stress leads to all manners of workplace ills, such as lowered team perspective, diminished desire to help others or solve problems, decreased motivation, and employee disengagement. Investing in employee wellness programs can increase overall employee happiness and workplace harmony, which leads to more engaged workers, less turnover, and many dollars saved.

Chapter 4

Your Voice Matters Because You Are Who You Are

"The tongue can paint what the eyes can't see"
~Chinese Proverb

15…. 16…. 17. That was exactly how many steps it took Sandy to get from the stairwell to her desk. She took off her coat, hung it on the knob on the side of her cubicle, and put her head down to work. Every day, she arrived almost a half hour early just so that she could avoid talking to other people and get a head start on the things on her to-do list for the day. She liked to work in silence, before everyone strolled in and started chatting with each other.

"Yeah, right," she thought as she looked up to pause at a noise. He's probably like the last owner who didn't want to hear anything except the word yes. She even remembered back to the old regime where one of the employees called off work at the last minute. The first shift employee was asked to do a double shift and when he said no, he was fired on the spot. That's what they were used to around here.

Yesterday's conversation with Mr. Davis hadn't changed her mind thoroughly. He seemed nice enough, but he didn't know anything about running a grocery store so what kind of ideas would he come up with about changing things? She was scared to even imagine it, much less voice her suggestions in the direction they should go.

Even in her last job before coming to the grocery store, Sandy didn't feel free to express herself. Management hadn't even let her take a weekend off for her sister to come into town. They just wouldn't listen. They didn't care. So, she learned to keep quiet, focus on her work and not cause any problems.

After graduating from college, she worked for one of the top accounting firms in the city. They had a strict dress code policy for the women to wear skirts, even in the winter. Back then, she was carpooling with other people to get to the South Side so they could share in the gas and parking costs to save money. They would all wait together outside the parking garage to grab the shuttle to their office building. On the way home, they'd do the same to get back.

Winters in Chicago were cold and standing in a skirt suit with a puffy coat, even with boots, was downright frigid. On top of it, there were nights they would stay late and waiting for the shuttle in the dark was pretty eerie. The company worked them long hours as recent graduates. It seemed like the company thought since they didn't have families yet, they could work 70-to-80-hour work weeks without a problem.

So, when she finally went to one of the partners and asked to wear pant suits instead, the other women were thrilled, but the male partners were not. At one of the staff meetings, she couldn't handle it anymore and blurted out, "I'll continue to wear a skirt every day when you stand out there in a skirt with me waiting for the shuttle!" Needless to say, when it came time for the standard two-year promotion, her colleagues moved up, but Sandy did not. She won the pantsuit fight but got punished for speaking up. She vowed she'd never sacrifice herself like that again.

It was a lot like her father used to tell her, "If you don't say anything, you can't get in trouble." So, for the many years following, she kept her mouth shut. Problem was, it often left her feeling disgruntled, unimportant and ignored. So, she ended up squashing all her feelings and thoughts down to try to ignore them, telling herself they weren't important or valid. So many times, in life, whether personal or business, she wished she would've had the nerve to say something. Instead, she worked on trying to let it go.

She was glad she reported directly to Mr. Davis now. Even though Matt seemed genuine, she was never sure if it was a front during the two years they'd already been working together. She had plenty of those colleagues who had acted like they cared but when she needed them, they disappeared. Besides, as a single mom, she'd figured out how to take care of herself. She didn't want any help; she could manage on her own. She had come this far without anyone swooping in to save her.

Every so often, Matt would come by and chat before giving her something she had asked for to complete her current project. It was nice, but she thought, "He has to be nice to me. I manage the numbers and send out the checks." Now, with Mr. Davis buying the grocery store, she was even more guarded. Though she wanted to trust him, she didn't know if she could.

Dad only wished that Sandy could understand what a great asset he felt she was. He tried to convey it and he could see past her guardedness -- he was intuitive like that. He was going to depend on her for the company forecasts and profit and loss statements. She'd be able to tell him which products were doing well, so he could order them again, and she could tell him which were underperforming as well. Her job was essential to growing the business and creating a wider profit spread. She had some great suggestions, but he noticed that during the meeting with upper management, it seemed as if Matt had to pry those ideas out of her. Dad pulled her aside afterward to let her know that he welcomed her feedback and if she didn't feel comfortable in a group setting, he would love to hear her thoughts any time. He had an open-door policy.

Through the conversations with the entire staff, Dad quickly recognized that Matt would be his right-hand man. Matt had really great managerial prowess. He was not the type of manager who would crush you if your idea wasn't feasible. The feedback from the other employees was glowing. Dad saw how Matt's team respected him. He communicated with his team and encouraged them to look at all sides, share their angle, and take the initiative to correct something before it became a major problem. He empowered them. Matt was the type of leader who wanted everyone in the grocery store to feel inspired by "failures" and never acted too busy to listen to a new idea.

Matt had even come up with an idea, on his own initiative, for Dad to inspire ideas and encourage buy-in. He proposed a contest in a "Plan our Future" session where they could all discuss the changes that would be coming up. He suggested that they either give just one prize or prizes for the top three. There could be prizes of a $100 award, a paid day off award, and a gift basket.

Kitchen Table Talks:

Dad had reflected on one of the chats he'd had with Sandy as he shared his day with Mom and the kids. He had finally gotten Sandy to open up today after many months and she mentioned that her former manager was extremely talkative. He would come to her cubicle and chat about nothing and waste time. If she needed him for something, he'd often talk about himself or his problems long before they got to business. She started to count the cracked bricks on the building outside their window or the number of woodgrain lines in his desk as he rambled on. Eventually, she learned to account for this extra time when they had meetings.

In time, Sandy became demotivated because her manager didn't seem to hear what she was saying. She was loyal, demonstrated ability and was considered a high performer on her yearly evaluations. However, she didn't feel valuable to the company because of this manager. She needed the paycheck and she enjoyed the work so she stayed, but when would she become the accounts manager rather than just a bookkeeper?

Dad knew he didn't want to manage the store like that. Employees needed to have a voice. If you hired the right people, you would want to hear what they had to say. Dad asked Mom if she could share how she developed her way of making you feel as though you were the most important person in the room and no one else but you mattered. That's what he wanted for the people at the grocery store.

· · · · · ·

What Obligation Do You Have to Use Your Voice?

It is not only management's responsibility to foster an EI culture that encourages EV, but it's also the employee's obligation to express themselves. Even though EV is a desirable outcome inside company culture, employees do not always want to share their thoughts. Because of this lack of communication, the leaders of your organization may have a problem understanding the issues occurring right in front of them. Generally speaking, employees don't always believe they have a say or that they'll be heard. They think that the decision-making process is not impacted by their input. For those who are truly in a culture that doesn't encourage them to speak up, they become more and more disengaged and disconnected from their workplace. They are hesitant to share any issues they encounter in their jobs, but if you are in the role of an employee, it's your obligation to use your voice in order to improve the culture you work in.

Leaders with EI who can effectively express themselves upwardly and downwardly in your organization are a great asset. Leaders have an even bigger obligation than employees to keep the channels of communication open. They create and maintain good relationships with their direct reports, as well as improve workplace productivity, and reduce turnover. Additionally, the conversations that open up improve team effectiveness and address project management concerns.

Why Your Voice Matters

When you speak up inside organizations, you create greater input and express opinions that can help the company. Managers who give employees the power to work together improve processes and systems in the workplace. The key to motivating your direct reports to use their voice lies in empowering them to be confident that their participation in the organization is respected and necessary.

Empathetic, motivated, and team-oriented people are generally emotionally intelligent employees and leaders who can communicate with others due to strong self-awareness and social skills. These skills are important to create and manage healthy relationships.

EI plays a role in facilitating your voice and the voice of the people you work with. When you can express yourself well and properly regulate your emotions, you can help someone else feel comfortable using their voice. The way you interact influences the reaction of the other person. If you, as a leader, react and respond favorably, employees tend to respond more favorably too. The level of EI in a company culture determines the quality of these exchanges and directly impacts the relationships throughout your organization.

How Can You Encourage Equality in Employee Voice?

If the leaders in your organization exhibit high EI, they can get their employees to be involved in projects no matter how difficult. When you genuinely care for those who work under you, you'll take the time to discuss their complaints. With an open-door policy, your employees can explain their concerns, as well as present any complaints. Your employees will feel like they are valued and involved in the decision-making procedures, rather than simply expected to follow instructions. When you can get employees to participate in this way, they become empowered in your workplace.

As the leaders and employees open up communication in your work culture, it's important to address relationship management too. This allows mutually beneficial exchanges to occur which further boosts EV throughout your organization. Relationship management involves the ability to collaborate with and develop other employees, as well as manage possible conflicts. This process offers a platform where employees can air their concerns, opinions, and ideas, thereby influencing the activities and decisions of the organization. This, in turn, helps to advance EV in a company.

Voice Equity

When you think of equality in the workplace, the first thing that may come to mind are gender differences. While this is a significant issue and is a leading driver for businesses to grow equality in the workplace, that is not the only area it involves. Equality means giving everyone the same respected treatment and opportunities, including but not limited to gender, abilities, and socio-economic status. It helps eliminate discrimination and develops an environment where every employee feels safe, unified, and equal with their peers.

If you already have established an equitable work culture or if you want to advance it even more, here are some guidelines that can help your organization.

1. **Put Equality Policies in Place**

Everyone should be treated fairly and valued for who they are each day when they come into work. Even if you strive to form an equitable culture, make sure you have official policies to back it up as well. Regardless of if it's purposely or not, a person's unconscious bias could leak through and cause concern. Having policies already in place to handle them is key to giving people more confidence and assurance that they are working in an environment that does not tolerate discrimination. Policies should include repercussions actions such as inexcusable language, gestures, stereotyping, and objectifying.

2.   Keep an Eye Out for Indirect Discrimination

Even if you have all your policies in place, sometimes they inadvertently and unintentionally place specific groups of people in a disadvantaged state. For example, a clean-cut rule could accidentally discriminate against someone's religion or make someone with a learning disability feel vulnerable. Furthermore, watch out for employees who make derogatory jokes. Even if they say they were kidding, it can be an indirect way for them to get away with discrimination and that should never be tolerated.

3.   Seek Help If Needed

Never feel ashamed if you come to recognize that you cannot handle transforming your organization's equality measures on your own. In fact, asking for help is one of the best things you can do. Your employees will certainly see you and your company in a more positive light for your committed efforts. The truth is that equality is a team effort.

Chapter 5
Diversity, Equity and Inclusion

"We are all different. Don't judge, understand instead."
~ Roy T. Bennett

Dad brought the whole company together for their bi-annual Diversity, Equity and Inclusion (DEI) meeting. This year he wanted the meeting to be more than just handing out papers and getting agreement about anti-bullying and acceptance of people who might be different from you. Even if you weren't technically in the currently protected groups, most people can relate to being treated as less than or being misunderstood. However, it can be hard to understand a perspective that you've never had to live through so Dad had asked some people inside and outside of the grocery store to share their experiences.

As the grocery store had grown in success, DEI had become more and more important to Dad, not only because it was a Black-owned store on the South Side of Chicago but because he had experienced it first-hand, even as the owner of the store. He wanted to encourage having open conversations to get to know someone on more than just a surface level. Some people have disabilities that are invisible. Others have disabilities that are physically evident as soon as you meet them. Oftentimes they don't know how to stand up for themselves or that if they do, they'll be persecuted.

Dad started the meeting by sharing that everyone has something that makes them different regardless of if it's officially something included in the Diversity, Equity and Inclusion discussion. Everyone is going through something in their life. It's our obligation to react in kindness, love and compassion because there's so much opportunity in embracing that we are all different for a reason.

He continued by sharing that DEI isn't only about making sure your organization has an official awareness program. Then he introduced his special guests to share their stories so that his employees could more fully understand their role in DEI no matter what their role is in the grocery store.

Phil

"Phil, your boyfriend is on the line," the receptionist had just popped into the break room to tell me I had a call. I could feel my face turn red and I quickly glanced around to see if anyone had noticed her word choice. This wasn't exactly how I had intended to come out to the whole office, but since it seemed like it didn't get much of a response from the people around me, I quickly corrected the receptionist by letting her know that I preferred the word, "partner."

That was in 1982, and at the time, I decided to immediately go to HR. I was still on my 12-week probationary period, and I was bracing myself for the boot. Much of my early career had been spent worrying and wondering what people would think of me being a gay man in small business. Would they stay away from me? Could I keep a job? Would they think that I was less than? What kind of comments would I get?

I remembered back to my first job at a temp agency, right before this position. There were two of us working the same position and in my naivety, I didn't realize that the other woman was collecting information on me. I have been known to be pretty chatty and she seemed "safe" so every day, I would share what my partner and I had done the previous day or weekend and she would share stories about her husband. I thought we were friends.

Because I was outperforming her, I realized later that she had probably concocted a plan to use these conversations against me. I got a call abruptly terminating me because, "We no longer need your services," even though I had had stellar performance reviews. They didn't have to give a reason, so I was confused for a long time. I didn't know what had happened until I reflected on it and recognized that sharing so openly with this woman may not have been the best idea. At that point, I vowed that I would not put it out there. That way, no one could use my sexual orientation against me.

Back at that time, it was hard for gay men to even rent an apartment. Discrimination was very high. AIDS was an epidemic. My partner and I wanted to get a simple one-bedroom apartment and a dozen places turned us down saying that two people of the same gender can't have a one-bedroom apartment, citing an ordinance against it in the city. That was the landscape.

Then this happened with the receptionist at my new job. I really thought I was going to lose my job. I thought it was the end again. So, I went to the manager's office and said, "I'm here to be terminated." To my surprise, the manager told me that my job was secure. I made a different vow to myself at that time that I would always come out in any future jobs because then they couldn't use it against me.

What I wish people knew about the LGBTQIA+ community is that there's a difference between acceptance and tolerance. The words mean quite distinctive things. If you accept someone, you're saying that you accept as they are, unconditionally. When someone says they tolerate you, they're saying that they're just putting up with you. As a community, we have a right to be accepted and many times we are not.

The next thing is around equal rights, not special rights. For example, gay couples were not allowed to get married for a long time. When we got that right, it wasn't a "special" right, it was an equal right. We don't ask for anything beyond what everyone is getting, but instead, we just want to have the same rights that others have.

Another thing that people don't understand is that there's a difference between sexual preference and sexual orientation. If it's a preference, it's implying that one day, I woke up and decided to be gay rather than straight. That's not what happens.

As an organization, I think that there should always be an Employee Resource Group in addition to the normal DEI awareness programs. This is a group created for anyone who is marginalized or on the fringe like LGBTQIA+ community, women, people of color, veterans, etc. This group gives these people the opportunity to create their mission, vision and values. And then they have a strategic plan on how they're going to create awareness and engagement around their communities and organizations with the purpose to increase the awareness around diversity, equity and inclusion.

Inside organizations, they should also try to actively model inclusivity. It's good that we have role models in high positions like Tim Cook, the CEO of Apple, Vice President Kamala Harris, or Michelle Obama for young black girls. We need people like this so that others can identify with them and be the right model because, not long ago, it was impossible for you to be openly gay or lesbian and be the CEO of a Fortune 500 company.

Organizations have a responsibility and accountability to create a safe space for their employees. That means no bullying or harassment is allowed, even as a "joke" or in ignorance, with or without intentional malice. Violence is at an all-time high and those who are working in your organization deserve to be protected in all ways -- verbally, emotionally, and physically. When an organization says that they have zero tolerance around this, you can expect to go into progressive disciplinary action. The employee may get a performance improvement plan and/or be terminated. When someone intends to be hurtful to another human, this is serious, and all organizations need to have a zero-tolerance policy in place that protects the organization and its individuals.

Frances

I couldn't believe what they were telling me.

They wanted me to be the front receptionist now that I got my cochlear implant and while my boss looked excited to tell me about my new responsibility, I wanted to crawl under the desk and cry. When I shared the situation with my other deaf friends, they understood. We didn't use normal phones. The last phone I had used before I lost my hearing was a rotary phone. Now that I had a cochlear implant, they thought I could handle answering and routing all the calls in the office?

I couldn't tell my boss how I was feeling or how terrified I was of picking up that phone with all the buttons. I didn't want to get fired. What was normal for other people wasn't normal for me. How did it work? I took a photo and sent it to a friend with normal hearing so that she could explain it to me. I had heard, "What's wrong with you? Are you stupid?" too many times in my life already.

The funny thing was that this phone issue had come around full circle. After college I had gotten a job in HR and one of my responsibilities was to conduct phone interviews. My hearing loss had happened gradually through childhood, into my teen and young adult life. The doctors had no definitive answer as to why I was losing my hearing, but the fact remained that I was going deaf. I was not doing well being in charge of phone interviews because I couldn't understand what people were saying so I went and applied for a job with Merry Maids. I thought cleaning offices by myself at night would be the perfect way to get away from my problems.

When I interviewed for the position, they asked me why I would leave a higher paying job which used my 4-year college degree to clean office buildings. I tried to make up a valid reason like wanting to eliminate stress, but it didn't work. I didn't get hired.

For 15 years before my cochlear implant, I had tried every type of new-fangled hearing aid to help me hear better, but none of them allowed me to hear clearly. I was still reading lips. In meetings it was hard to understand everyone, especially if people were talking at the same time or if there was someone having a side conversation in the background. Parties were even worse. The hum of the music or chatter would make it hard for me to concentrate on the person right in front of me. Sometimes I would ask people to repeat what they said, and they'd shrug it off, wave their hand and say, "I wasn't important." This small thing is what the hearing world doesn't understand because it always left me feeling unimportant as well. If you couldn't take two seconds to repeat yourself, then I must not matter very much.

Outside of work, I'd try to hide it. I was ashamed and embarrassed. My self-esteem and self-worth were in the toilet because I felt flawed and broken. I tried not to interact in public. There were times I wished I could be like some of the women in my support group -- the few who demanded their accommodations and cited the Americans with Disabilities Act (ADA). But the majority of us just don't want to call attention to ourselves. We wanted to do our jobs and not cause any waves.

Janine

As I opened the door to the conference room, the meeting host looked up from the long mahogany table and asked, "Is your boss on her way?" This wasn't the first time this had happened. I had even straightened my hair instead of wearing it in braids or au naturel. I guess it's sometimes hard for a White males or females to imagine that their boss hired a Black woman to teach them how to speak more eloquently, present better, and to confidently stand in front of a room.

It definitely wasn't uncommon because over the past weekend, I had gotten together with some of my friends for dinner. Two of them were doctors, also Black women, who worked at a hospital where they were paid less than their counterparts. I listened to them as they lamented promotions that should've been theirs. Many of their male colleagues rose through the ranks at a much faster speed than they did, and it was tiring to watch it happen over and over again. It was also hard for them to find great mentors or to mentor new doctors when it was evident the hospital was not interested in diversifying their pool of doctors.

Our one Asian friend would share stories that there were

stereotypes of Asians. Sometimes the assumption of being intelligent worked to her advantage but being a woman stockbroker amongst "The Good Ole Boys," as she called them, was difficult. She had to prove herself over and over. It was even more important for her to be at the top of the sales leader board and once, in a meeting, one of the male stockbrokers had said, "Oh, it's easy for you. Just set up a kiosk in a mall and wear a short skirt and you'll have a ton of new clients in no time." The manager didn't even put this guy in his place. Instead, the whole room laughed and agreed. As if that type of new client would've been ideal.

I was taught by my older sister about how to act in public. She always warned me that when she went into a store, she made sure not to put her hands in her purse or carry a large tote. If she did, she took her wallet out before entering the store so that no one there would think she was trying to steal something.

There were times when I would drive through town and randomly get pulled over by a police officer because a Black woman couldn't possibly own an Audi. I always made sure my husband knew where I was going and by what route just in case. Sometimes I would call him as I took a turn onto a side road just to see if the police officer was tailing me on purpose. Even my three kids have a lawyer on speed dial in their contacts in case they ever need the help.

Now as I am becoming a leader in my field, I'm still up against the prejudices that society has believed for many centuries. There had been times that people had gone to HR after a meeting saying that I had been "too aggressive" but, when the White man stood up and said the same thing and his voice got deeper, he was just passionate and assertive. What he was saying was commanding attention. All too often the "angry Black woman" stereotype follows me around, making me feel like I need to tone it down to a whisper.

Oftentimes, racist people are creating the systems that we work in. The creators of the policies that are being put into place are racist, so it becomes a systemic issue. Just because you hire one token Black woman for a management position, it doesn't absolve your company from any more responsibility. All too often, organizations think they don't need to be a part of the conversation anymore.

But here's the thing, I don't want you to hire me because I'm a Black woman and you need to fill a quota. I want to be hired because I'm qualified and equipped. Once I'm in your organization, I want to be treated equally. What's hard is how to define equal when you're talking to someone who doesn't experience discrimination in the same way.

Kitchen Table Talks:

Dad, Matt and Sandy had a meeting of the minds after the DEI company meeting. Dad said he wished he had invited these stories and conversations earlier. Even as a Black man owning a business, he experienced things differently than what these guests had shared. It had been an eye-opening, mind-opening experience.

That night over dinner, Dad shared all the stories with Mom. The two kids, now teens, were pretending not to listen, but the stories were way too interesting. They ended up sharing some of the bullying and other incidents that had happened in school -- ones that had happened to them and others from friends or people they didn't really know.

In particular, there was a story about an interracial couple who had been picked on from the very beginning. They had tried to keep the relationship a secret at first, but it eventually became too evident in school. Both sides were giving them a hard time about being together. The girl was White, the boy was Black, and she tried to tell the boy's friends that she wasn't racist because she was dating someone Black. However, just because you're in a relationship with someone of another race doesn't mean you're not racist. She had a hard time defending herself because she lacked the perspective of being Black.

Mom said, "The battle is the Lord's, and we also need to do our part." Dad and the kids agreed, so one of the first things Dad was going to do was put together that Employee Resource Group to support the current DEI program. He knew it had to start at the top. It was his goal to become the foremost business example in Chicago with programs that would further DEI, not just give it lip service. In his mind, he was saying what he always said to the kids, "Don't settle for second. You've already won first."

• • • • • •

Building, managing, and maintaining diversity within your business or company can be quite the challenge, but certainly a necessary one. Not only will it boost your reputation as a company, but it also shows that you are playing an active part to foster positive change and acceptance in the world. That is powerful all on its own and future generations will benefit from it. From people with disabilities (PWDs), age, gender, sexual orientation, political views, cultural background, religion, race, to ethnicity, everyone is unique in their own way and offers immense value. Growing your small business culture to welcome everyone should be a primary goal, especially in regard to recognizing and appreciating the humanity and dignity of another person.

Diversity, equity, and inclusion in the workplace are some of the most discussed topics in Human Resources. Research suggests diversity, just like EI and EV, has positive results on productivity, creativity and innovation, decision-making, employee morale, and sales and profits. Unfortunately, even when employers and firms in small business diversify purposefully, they see little progress in their culture because the policies and programs are not effective.

What's the difference between diversity, equity, and inclusion? The terms are often mixed and used interchangeably, which presents a huge misunderstanding and wrong perception when practiced.

What is diversity?

When a workplace is diverse, it accepts and values differences between people of different ethnicities, genders, ages, religions, disabilities, and sexual orientations. Not only that, but it also encompasses differences in knowledge, skills, education, and personalities. Diversity is often the first phase of the DEI concept.

What is inclusion?

Even if you have your diverse pool of talents, there's no guarantee that the workplace will be able to appreciate and accept them. Inclusion is about welcoming the involvement, presence, and ideas of every team member and their EV. Without inclusion, an organization's diversity program can turn lackluster.

What is equity?

After welcoming your diverse team in the company, you need to ensure that everyone has equal opportunities for resources, pay, training, and support systems. Examples of equity situations you can tackle are:

1. Are promotions limited only to abled employees? How about people with varied abilities?
2. Do you have gender sensitivity programs that are also inclusive of all employees in the workplace?
3. Do any older employees feel as though they lag

behind in education or training for company technology and innovation?

If you can embrace these three factors in your organization, your programs will get greater results and your company's bright prospects will advance faster.

Why Does an EI Small Business Culture Need Diversity, Equity, and Inclusion?

Too often, diversity and inclusion are practiced without an equity basis. When the three are combined, your workforce is empowered to greater innovation and productivity. That's because equity offers your diverse team equal opportunities and a well-levelled playing field. It also allows for important points of view that you may not otherwise be privy to.

Diversity x Equity

If your company is open to diversity and opportunities in the workplace, but lacks inclusion, the employee might feel distant and dismissive. For instance, higher and equal pay in a company doesn't compensate for the respect, employee engagement, and the feeling of belongingness in the firm.

Diversity x Inclusivity

Without equity, your organization may lack depth-dimensional leadership, good problem-solving approaches, and high employee morale. For instance, if minority groups in a company such as women of color, PWDs, LGBTQI+, baby boomers, etc., feel unheard, it can lead to dissatisfaction and attrition.

Equity x Inclusivity

Without diversity, your organization limits itself from opportunities over the preference of a collective whole. Diversity allows for more creative innovation, fresh ideas, and new perspectives.

If your company is planning to launch diversity, equity and inclusion (DEI) initiatives in the workplace, consider your internal practices and personal biases.

Statistics prove that there's a growing demand for DEI initiatives. According to Glassdoor, a company review website, workplace diversity accounts for 67% of job seekers' consideration when searching for employment opportunities.

Among the respondents are:
- 19.3% are PWDs
- 70% are Latinos
- 72% are women
- 80% are Asians
- 89% of African Americans

If employers refuse to include DEI in their programs, they miss out in the talent pools and lose out on prospective opportunities.

According to Culture Amp, 40% of employees feel left out in the business decision-making process which leads to resignation. The results of the survey found it unfortunate enough since women often bring some of the best ideas to the table.

That study is backed up by another study by Fast Company that found women in C-suite level positions provide 34% higher yields of returns on investment.

DEI initiatives also provide the following results:
1. Diverse teams outperform norm-tendency teams by 87%.
2. Diverse companies outperform competitors in the industry by 35%.
3. Firms with high inclusion of diverse teams had 19% growing revenues.
4. Businesses with 2D diversity captured new markets by 45% and have entered about 70% of the industry as well.
5. Companies improved their creations, works, and services by 27% with diverse teams.

So, why shouldn't you include this great talent pool in your company? It's been shown that companies rich in diversity, equity, and inclusion are the ones that usually succeed.

How is a Diversity, Equity and Inclusion Workplace Achieved?

Diversity doesn't end in the hiring process. In reality, it

begins when your employees embrace themselves as a part of your organization. To create a successful DEI program, this has to be an executive strategy. Too often HR managers find themselves implementing these initiatives with only 65% of senior executives believing it's not their job to promote and participate.

If you want to create change in the workplace, here are the next steps:

1. Collect and compile data.

Know what your company is like by collecting and compiling data from your employees. You can study and understand better how diversity affects your organization through internal practices.

You can start by knowing your current employee pool:
1. Age
2. Ability
3. Race and ethnicity
4. Gender identity or sexual orientation
5. Language
6. Educational background
7. Personality type

Companies don't need to snoop around their files. You can even gather all your employees' activity and let them introduce themselves. It's a way of gauging their reactions, thoughts, and personality naturally.

2. Identify and analyze areas of concern.

Analyze the representation of diversity, inclusion, and equity on your team. Ask yourselves of these questions:

1. Are we hiring diverse enough teams?
2. Is this department hiring only male employees? Do you have any programs such as STEAM for women?
3. Are the management leaders and decision-makers all males?

These areas of concern can be discussed within the management level, HR department, or, for smaller companies, within your groups.

3.   Address policies, practices, and company objectives.

Discuss policies, practices, and company objectives that hinder employment and rewards opportunities. Include the following practices:

1. Implement a benefits and rewards program.
2. Provide training on personal biases in departments.
3. Enhance company culture and engagement
4. Improve company training and informational workshops about DEI initiatives.
5. Create support systems for PWDs' assistance, gender harassment, and racial discrimination.

4. **Create SMARTIE objectives.**

Create specific, measurable, attainable, realistic, and time-bound objectives for your DEI initiatives. For example: to increase diverse employee morale for higher productivity and profits within 6 months.

- Specific: Increase diverse employee morale
- Measurable results: employee productivity, morale, turnover, attendees, absentees, and retention
- Attainable: with diverse teams
- Realistic: employee morale and workmanship
- Time-bound: 6 months
- Inclusive
- Equitable

5. **Implement the initiatives.**

What activities and programs can you include for your DEI initiatives? It's also important to include the executive and management level when implementing policies, programs, and initiatives. For example:

1. Create monthly training and outreach for the company.
2. Invest in technology for PWDs.
3. Change in the hiring process.
4. Assess penalties in discrimination.
5. Provide mental health support.
6. Conduct performance and business reviews.
7. Offer opportunities for bonuses, salary

increases, and promotions.

6.   Measure the program.

To understand how your programs are geared for success, measure the results of the DEI initiatives. That way, you'll know that your programs are implemented effectively. You can measure your programs effectiveness through:

1.   Employee retention metrics
2.   Company productivity reports
3.   Employee morale and turnover outcomes
4.   Attendees and absentees' records
5.   Happiness engineering results

7.   Review, evaluate, and repeat.

DEI requires continuous work in response to the changing needs of the company. The firm must create a regular review of the programs, then adapt, change, and initiate the programs accordingly.

A Special Note for People with Learning Disabilities

Up to ten percent of the population is affected by some form of learning disability, including dyslexia, autism, and dyscalculia. Additionally, about seven percent of the adult US population is clinically depressed, which is a psychiatric disability covered and protected under the Americans with Disabilities Act. Since it is up to the employee to share this with an employer, there is a good chance that many will keep it to themselves as a way to avoid being a target for harassment or discrimination. So, what can you do about this as an employer?

1. Set strict policies in place that have associated punishments for those who discriminate or make jokes involving mental health or disabilities of any kind.
2. Monitor your employee's performances and if you see someone struggling, consider giving them some extra support or pairing them up in a role that better highlights their strengths.
3. Offer flexible time off or remote working opportunities that can appeal to those who may need to step away from the traditional environment once in a while.
4. Foster an equal, diversified, and inclusive culture where everyone has the freedom to speak their opinions and perspectives and is respected for doing so.
5. Collaborate with an external mental health and/or disability professional and promote around your workplace to create an Employee Assistance Plan (EAP). This gives people the ability to partake and share in a private space outside of work if they wish without interacting with co-workers or management.

Put policies in place, provide alternative options, and have one-on-one meetings with your employees to see if they are struggling or not to help them along. These are all excellent things you can do to grow an outstanding working environment and really make those with hidden disabilities feel more unified, supported, and an integral part of the overall team. Even if they never come out and tell you what is going on inside of them, you can guarantee that your efforts will not go unnoticed, and they will certainly be appreciated.

Remember also that not every disability can be seen with the naked eye. In addition, not every diagnosis is physically debilitating or entirely disables a person from being able to become a valuable resource to an organization. Differences, including, but not limited to learning differences, color-blindness, depression, autism, anxiety, and PTSD, are all things someone can have that might not be obvious they are carrying. Furthermore, PWDs may "look like" every other person going about their day. Therefore, it can be all too easy to assume that they are not struggling day to day. Because you will never know what someone may be holding inside, creating an all-inclusive workplace helps empower them and gives them encouragement to use their voice.

1. **Establish A Company Culture Where Every Voice is Welcomed and Respected**

People tend to quit their jobs when they feel like they cannot be their authentic selves and embrace their uniqueness. Because of this, take a look at your workplace culture and strengthen it to become more appreciative, value-oriented, and connected for everyone. Give your employees the ability to freely express themselves and their personal perspectives regarding their race, religion, gender, etc. You can do this by celebrating every holiday, not playing favorites, and demonstrating that there is no backlashing or victimization for voicing concerns or opinions.

2. **Review Policies**

Dive into your policies with a diversity lens. Do you see any loopholes or something too ambiguous that can be interpreted as non-inclusive? For example, maybe you have recreational activities for your employees that are not favored for those who have learning disabilities or goes against a particular religion. Or perhaps your policies are not beneficial to breastfeeding mothers even though you fulfill the basic requirements that are legally covered (i.e. flexible pumping breaks). No matter what it is, make changes where you see necessary that appeals to everyone. You can always have a lawyer help you as well, so you do not miss anything critical.

3. **Leverage Diverse Job Boards**

Even if you have the best, diversified workplace, it will not do much good if you only hire the same type of people. Because diversity begins with the hiring process, think about leveraging diverse job boards such as Diversity Working, Hire Autism, and Recruit Disability to get your job requisitions in the hands of a more varied audience. This will enable more people who are different to apply overall and help you grow a diverse culture.

As you can see, there are several things you can do to

alter your business views, both internally and externally, to promote diversity. Though they are all little aspects that might need to be tweaked, never underestimate the potent ability those small transformations can make. If you do your due diligence and put in the time to optimize your business or company for all-inclusion, your efforts will collectively pay off in the end. Though these alterations might not show results overnight, be patient and know that every step you take will have massive impacts in the long run, both within society and for your business prosperity as well.

Chapter 6

Achieving Your High EI Small Business Culture

"It doesn't make sense to hire smart people and then tell them what to do;
we hire smart people so they can tell us what to do."
~ Steve Jobs

He was jumping up and down shouting, "Open sesame!" but the doors just didn't seem to notice he was there.

Roy remembered back when he would visit Dad at the grocery store after school. He couldn't remember a time when he wasn't excited to go there. At first, he barely weighed enough to get the automatic doors to open. Sometimes he had to jump and stomp to get the doors to magically slide to greet him.

At first, Dad didn't want Roy to come to the store too often. After all, he had invested in the store so that he could give the kids a life he never had. He didn't want them to return after private school and college to run the store. He wanted them to go their own way and do great things.

But Roy had grown up listening to Mom and Dad talk around the kitchen table. At first, he didn't understand it all, but he slowly, silently caught on to their conversations.

Soon, he was begging to come by the store after school. Sometimes he would stack cans on the end cap into a triangular tower. Kristin always let him sit on the counter as she checked out the customers and he enjoyed bagging the customer's groceries from his perch. When he'd go upstairs to the office, Sandy would let him play with her adding machine. That was his favorite, but of course, now they don't use such things. He used to love watching the ticker tape print out the important numbers he had "calculated" to take and report to his dad. Matt always called him "slugger" and asked him what he was learning in school.

Roy would pretend that he was conducting meetings in the big meeting room at the end of the hall. He would grab a stack of paper to be recycled from the copy room and stand at the head of the table giving a presentation to his "team" who were represented by the framed pictures of his mom, sister, and brothers that he took from Dad's office desk. As he grew older, the table seemed to shrink and soon it was time to go to college.

He had learned a lot about business, communication, relationships, and people. Every night Dad would chat with Mom over dinner. It interested him so much that he studied business at Duke University. Dad had actually tried to talk him out of buying the grocery store from him, but Roy insisted he had great ideas for expansion and legacy. Dad knew there was no talking him out of it. Truth be told, he was proud of Roy coming back home. It was nice to have him around again. Now, two months shy of the store's 25th anniversary, Dad was handing the keys over to him.

This time walking into the grocery store felt different. Roy wasn't three feet tall anymore trying to get the glass doors to notice him and open up. He stood six foot two, former athlete, husband and father of three children. He looked forward to having them visit him here after school like he once did.

Sandy had spent her whole career at the grocery store. She had seen a lot of changes and employees come and go, but she wasn't sure she wanted to adapt to a new boss again. It had taken her a lot of time to finally trust Dad. Roy had been gone for a number of years and had only been at the store as a kid. Sure, he helped out as a teen wherever his dad told him to fill in, but could he, do it? Even the other places he had worked before didn't make her feel better. All Sandy was worried about was if things were going to change for the better or for the worse. Would he change up her processes? Would they work well together? Even though she had watched him grow up, would Roy keep her around or replace her with someone younger?

Kitchen Table Talks:

It felt like a special day when Dad and Roy came home for dinner. Mom and Roy's wife, Carolyn, were busy making dinner when they arrived home, talking about the business plan as they opened the door. "One of the things I wish I would've done right away was make a business plan," Dad told Roy, but this wasn't the first time Roy had heard this story. He grinned as Dad recounted, yet again, the early days of owning the grocery store.

Roy shared with Dad that he wanted to give people the opportunity to better themselves. It was important that as the grocery store grew, the people were growing personally and business-wise too. Roy intended to get an organization to come in and do a 3rd party assessment. He also had ideas of offering a way for the employees to take classes for free on a variety of topics. He had seen from his previous jobs -- when you lead from an others-centered vision, there is more success, and it comes faster and easier for an organization. There is a high return for creating opportunities for people by believing in their assets.

Dad went through the employee list off the top of his head pointing out each person's strong points. He also talked about those who were dependable – the ones who always showed up or stayed late in a pinch. There had also been some employees who had come and gone who weren't committed and there were some people who had great skills, but they didn't fit into the store's business model or mission.

Now Dad wanted to quiz Roy. He asked, "How do you relate to someone that you don't have anything in common with?"

Roy answered by saying, "I think there's a larger question here. Do you listen to your employees? Anyone can do that. You need to seek to understand their perspective through listening."

Roy continued by sharing that there was a distinct difference between relationship management and relating. Having a relationship with someone is important but that doesn't mean that a person can relate. In management, aside from assessing and developing strategies, one of the most important things a business leader does is create those relationships. When you think of long-term visions and goals, a leader needs to think about people, relationships, and team. It's one of the primary responsibilities. That creates loyalty.

Their conversation overtook the dinnertime topic, but Mom and Carolyn didn't mind. They were used to it by now and Roy and Carolyn's kids had scampered off to play while they were finishing up.

As they moved to the family room couch, Dad said, "Son, remember: Don't let nothing kill your faith. Don't let nothing kill your confidence. And never do anything you don't want your mom to find out about." Mom chuckled and said, "That's right because I've got eyes everywhere, even in the back of my head."

• • • • • •

Why Change is Important

When people feel like they're either underpaid, mistreated, misunderstood or not valued, what do they do? They take the stapler home. They take the envelopes home; they use the company postage meter. They try to make up for how they feel about working there especially if they don't feel like there's a sense of justice. They will attempt to "level the playing field" by trying to create it in their own way.

Even companies already operating in a highly emotionally intelligent culture will have to look at constant improvements to maintain the best working environments. It's easy to get comfortable when the company culture is working well, but in order to keep employees motivated, you must continue to seek ongoing excellence.

Aside from the obvious reasons to implement positive change, the workplace is constantly changing with the changing world. It wasn't too long ago that women were a much smaller minority in the workforce. It also wasn't too long ago that people with disabilities were institutionalized rather than employed. Who knows what the future will bring, but one thing is for certain: change will be necessary in order to keep up. Organizations that refuse to change will be left behind and replaced by those who implement quickly and embrace new ideas.

As mentioned before, the higher the EI of the leaders in your organization, the more EV is encouraged. This is why creating a highly emotionally intelligent culture is important. Aside from being collaborative, high EI leaders are also more adaptable. This means that they can easily acclimatize to new ideas and solutions presented by your employees. Highly emotionally intelligent leaders have been found to be empowering as well. They promote collaboration and are not afraid to share their power with their employees. Being collaborative, trusting, adaptable, and empowering are just some of the traits that come with high EI. These traits encourage EV which, in turn, helps encourage positive change.

How to Navigate the Change

Transitions, change, and getting unstuck from old ways to make room from the new can be a challenge. You may really feel like your systems, operations, or methodology need to improve, but getting started can feel a lot like trying to navigate a dark maze while blindfolded. The good news is, anything is possible, even if it doesn't feel like it at the moment. With commitment, leveraging your authenticity, and streamlining your focus, you will discover that every small step in the right direction will lead you, your organization, and your employees to exactly where you need to be.

Some of your employees or leaders may resist change, but change is neither good or bad, right or wrong. It just is.

Evaluate

Take some time to evaluate what is or is not working in your organization. Write it down, brainstorm, and find common trends that can be traced back to the root cause. Once you pinpoint the underlying issue, you can work on remediating it. Before that, you will be just shooting in the dark and getting frustrated.

Come Up with a Transition Timeline

Construct a timeline with milestone goals along the way that your organization can aim for. These little celebratory goal moments are all puzzle pieces that create the big picture and help you transform for the better.

Work on Improving Yourself

In order to make any business changes, start from within. Change begins and ends with you, so make sure you prioritize yourself. Regardless of the stage you are in and what your goals are, it is vital to never stop striving for more and diving deep inside yourself to see what's possible. Who knows, you may have only scratched the surface. Remember, you are brilliant, and the best of you is waiting to be revealed.

How EI Contributes to Positive Change

Studies have shown that EI affects job satisfaction and stress management. Interestingly enough, similar studies have found that job satisfaction is also related to EV. As the leaders of your organization manage several, diverse individuals, their role may require a specific type of EI or an emphasis on a specific component of EI directed at people. People are social creatures by nature, so relationships and interactions, among other social functions, are important. Relationship management is the mechanism that encourages EV the most and high EI individuals are more likely to form positive relationships with the people around them.

When you employ highly emotionally intelligent individuals, it also helps to decrease workplace ostracism, which reflects better relationships. This means that high EI leaders make employees feel welcome and supported in your organization. Enhanced relationships between leaders and employees, fostered by the leaders' relationship management, has been shown to be highly valued by employees as an avenue for their career growth, where they can share their creative ideas.

It is not enough for the leaders in your organization to simply be engaged in the workplace to inspire members to do the same. They must have real relationships with the employees if they want to inspire them to do the same amongst themselves. When employees are more engaged, they are more inclined to use EV to create change and improve their work. High EI managers are able to correctly identify their employees' emotional needs and act as supportive mentors. High EI leaders are also able to think of creative ways to reward employees for their contributions, which encourages EV even more.

When EI is used in teams, it promotes a deeper and more efficient understanding of tasks and, more importantly, an exchange of diverse ideas inside the team that lead to positive change.

On an even bigger scale, your leaders' EI may also influence organizational climate. This is accomplished by nurturing an environment of high expectations and self-confidence which makes the workplace more attractive. When you have a company culture built on high EI, it cultivates trust, information sharing, healthy risk-taking, and growth. In contrast, low EI leaders form a culture built on fear and anxiety, which lowers the chance of EV since employees would be too anxious to lose their jobs or receive repercussions if they shared ideas on how to create positive change.

It's important to note that some of your leaders may not accurately judge their own level of EI which makes it difficult for them to utilize it. For instance, if a leader believed that he had high EI when he did not, he might misread certain employee behaviors and react inappropriately and squelch open communication with his employees. There is also the idea that if you have employees with high EI, they will encourage their own EV. Some studies even point to the employees' EI as more important than their manager's EI in encouraging EV and open communication for positive change.

Chapter 7

Momentum Mirror Moments for Change (M3C)

"The greatest discovery of all time is that a person can change his future by merely changing his attitude."
~ Oprah Winfrey

Sandy peered closely into the mirror as she thought, "Great, another grey hair." She saw more crow's feet around her eyes and dabbed concealer under her eyes to hide the circles underneath. Yesterday the doctor told her that she was pre-diabetic. That had not come as much of a surprise because, four years ago, her mother died from diabetes and her two siblings were taking insulin shots. Sandy had tried to do better with eating, but sometimes life just seemed to warrant a box of cookies or a bowl of ice cream.

She thought back to the 29 years she had worked for Mr. Davis at the grocery store. She had never intended to stay there that long. Her daughter was grown up now, had even gotten married, now with a small child of her own.

Thirty years ago, Sandy thought she would've remarried again too, maybe even had more children but that's not how life turned out. After her daughter's father left them, Sandy poured herself into work. It was easier to concentrate on that. She liked it best if people at the office left her alone and just let her do her thing. Everyone at the office knew her as the dedicated quiet one and she liked it that way, even though Matt and Mr. Davis both tried to have conversations with her.

Every once in a while, one of her friends would try to set her up with a date, but most of them ended up being frogs. She even tried a few dating apps – swipe left, swipe right, she hadn't had any luck except for Mike. He seemed to have potential but, in the end, they agreed they both had baggage that they couldn't get past, and they knew it wasn't going to work out. She wanted more kids, even quitting her job and staying home with them, but he had two children from a previous marriage and didn't want to have any more. It was a fundamental difference they just couldn't get past.

So here she was now 57 years old, all alone. Should she have made a different choice? It wasn't that she lived a bad life. In fact, she could point out a lot of things that had worked out well. She had a job she enjoyed, in an organization where she felt valued. Even though she was quiet, Mr. Davis always pulled her aside to hear her views. She watched little Roy grow up and could honestly say, after some initial reservations, that she was happy he was taking things over. It would be good to get some younger perspectives for the grocery store.

But Sandy kept wondering if this was all there was to life. She had put on the pounds slowly and every New Year made a resolution to go to the gym and eat better. Most nights, she had a hard time sleeping and she worried about the unending list of things to do every day at work and at home. There was pressure to do her job well. She didn't want to get replaced by a younger, faster version. At home, there always seemed to be something that needed to be done whether it be re-caulking the bathtub or just cleaning the kitchen.

Thing was, it seemed like every day was starting to blend into the other. She would try to sleep in over the weekends but would inevitably wake up early. At least her daughter and her family would come over from time to time and they got to talk on the phone on a regular basis. There was one thing she had done right. Her daughter was still her everything.

Sandy knew that she needed to make some changes though. And as she finished putting on her eyeliner, she made a vow to be the woman she'd always wanted to be – bolder, speaking her mind, feeling energetic and healthy. She opened the drawer and started to pull out the lipstick she wore every day when she spied an old tube she had bought on a whim. It was bright red. Was she crazy? What would people think at the office? She was always so muted; she wanted to just fade in. Maybe today was the day she would start standing out. Slowly she opened the tube and applied the lipstick. "This weekend I'm going to get my hair dyed too," she thought to herself, "Yes, it's going to be a new beginning."

Kitchen Table Talks:

Dad looked at Mom across the kitchen table. So many conversations had happened right here. The table itself had grown older with them with marks and dents from the kids giving it character. There were sparkles that their daughter had glued that somehow never came off and permanent markers from school projects here and there. The kids grew up at this table, listening to the talks, sometimes the disagreements, and many times the belly laughs that made them cry. Now their grandchildren would come over and take those same chairs, spilling the same cups, dropping more crumbs underneath the table.

Dad reached over and took Mom's hand and asked her, "Would you have done anything differently?"

• • • • • •

In business and in life we are constantly growing, and an organization needs to acknowledge each employee's need for this growth. If your employees aren't growing, you're stunting the company's growth as well. You need to encourage your team to spread their wings and fly because if your employee is the same person when they enter your organization as when they leave your organization, you've missed out on a great opportunity.

What is Momentum Mirror Moments for Change (M3C)?

It begins with us, how we see ourselves, and who we are called to be. Momentum Mirror Moments for Change (M3C) are those times in our lives when we look in the mirror and we ask ourselves who we are. Is this the person in the mirror, the person I want to be and am I who I'd thought I'd be at this particular stage in my life? Many times, M3C happens at major times in life like when your child is graduating from preschool or high school or when you're turning a particular age. It's times when you look at yourself in the mirror, identify where you are, evaluate where you thought you'd be, and ask yourself where you want to go.

Why is M3C important?

There are times in life when you pause and consider whether who you are at this stage in life or age is who you thought you'd be. It's important to see these moments as opportunities rather than obstacles. If you're not who or where you want to be, it's easy to get upset or have regrets. Just know that you are not a victim. You are an empowered person who can set the course for your life. That's why M3C is important to consciously experience. Through these times, you can be encouraged and strengthened to live life more intentionally.

How do you implement M3C in your life?

Step 1: Assess

Look in a full-length mirror and ask yourself what you see. Describe it in detail from a physical, emotional, mental, environmental and spiritual perspective.

Step 2: Evaluation

Next ask yourself what you feel about what you see. What do you think of what you see? Why does it matter?

While it's true that it doesn't matter what other people think, from the perspective of personal and organizational change, as social beings, it matters how we interact with each other. From that respect, as someone working in a team, you need to know what other people think of you. In that way, you can interact better with the people in your organization.

Ask yourself how you show up on a daily basis. Then ask yourself how you show up under stress. How do people perceive you in that situation? Is it accurate to what you want to portray?

Step 3: Transformation

Just like a butterfly emerges from a cocoon as a new creature, you can do the same. Ask yourself who you desire to be. This is what we call the Ideal Destination. And as you grow and change, this can change as well. But for each M3C, ask yourself what needs to be addressed in order for you to be who you want to be and how you want to be seen by others. How can you be a better boss, employee, friend, and family member?

During this step, you may be required to take off your mask. You'll want to set goals to get to your Ideal Destination. Now is the time to be brutally honest with yourself. Who do you want to be? It's not about what your mother or father wanted for you or what your friends expect from you. It's not what a teacher once said to you. It's not even about who your spouse thinks you should be. It's about what you want for yourself.

Step 4: Evolution

M3C is not a one and done process. It's an ongoing thing that happens many times in a person's life. Who you decide you want to be at age 20 may change through the years and maybe at age 23 you realize you want something else. By the time you're 40, maybe your priorities have changed, but you couldn't have predicted that at age 23. So, don't feel like you get to choose once and that's it. You get to use this process to evolve.

You also have to make a decision about what you're willing to do to get to your Ideal Destination. This part is about honesty because you can surely desire something, but then also not be willing to make the necessary changes to get there. It's neither wrong nor right. You just have to decide how much it means to you and if you're willing to make the modifications to your life to get there.

This is also where emotional intelligence and employee voice come together. What you choose impacts other people and vice versa. How you change will change how others relate to you. It will dictate how you show up, what your views about certain topics are and how you view other people in the world.

Sometimes the changes you make feel minor and

sometimes they appear major. You may surprise some people who normally expect you to act or react a specific way like you have in the past. They might feel your responses are out of character until they get used to the new you. Expect this as you break your old mold.

Most people can't get through M3C completely by themselves so one of the most helpful things to do for M3C is to have someone help you through the journey. Sometimes you can't see something that they do. They can be the mirror for you. Other times you may want to change, but don't know how and they can help you achieve it.

When people feel stuck, it's often because they are looking for some sort of momentum to get them out of it. Most of the time, we are not looking to pace ourselves little by little to achieve the change slowly. People want that shift to occur as soon as possible once they've identified their Ideal Destination.

If you want to implement M3C in your life, you have to be ready. You need to want to look in that mirror, make the assessment and follow the rest of the process. And with the momentum to make the changes, you can experience exponential growth which then will lead to exponential results.

Chapter 8
Managing Emotions in Your Workplace

"It's through curiosity and looking at opportunities in new ways that we've always mapped our path."
~ Michael Dell

Matt almost slammed the door closed to Dad's office as he sat down in the leather armchair. He wasn't usually like this, so Dad knew something was up. They had come to an agreement over the years to always speak their minds and not be worried about sugar coating the details.

"What's wrong?" Dad asked.

"It's my new assistant Rebecca," Matt said. "She keeps overlapping my meetings and messing up my calendar."

Matt gave Rebecca both his office and his personal calendars and asked her to be mindful of the two schedules when she booked his meetings. There were obligations that couldn't overlap and buffer times that needed to be taken into account in case anything ran over. Regularly, she would create impossible schedules where there was no drive time, let alone a bathroom break. He repeatedly asked her to correct this problem, but it was as if she wasn't listening.

"I feel like I have to give her step-by-step instructions and she can't think on her own. It's as if she can't conceptualize this or ask me if there's a question. I have to tell her every single thing she has to do and consider. In that case, I might as well do it on my own!"

Dad could see the emotions bubble over as Matt continued to vent his frustrations.

"You know me … I'm usually a pretty chill guy, but Rebecca is really testing my fortitude. On top of that, I'm losing my patience when I talk to her and I'm sure I'm coming off as a jerk."

Dad glanced out the glass window of his office to the cubicles down the hall. He could see Rebecca grabbing a tissue and turning her chair to face the wall.

For Rebecca, this was just another time this month when Matt, her new boss, was upset with her. Couldn't he see she was doing the best she could? She had lost her previous job when the company she had been working for went bankrupt and because her family depended on her paycheck, she took the first thing that she could. It wasn't exactly what she wanted, and she wished she didn't have those bills, the student loans or the credit card debt. Then maybe she would have looked longer or had better choices. She was a college graduate. Couldn't Matt see she was way more than an assistant?

The calendar was a menial task. She could be helping

Matt with bigger projects, but he didn't seem to want to collaborate with her even when she suggested it. After all, she saw his whole calendar, all his projects and due dates. The fact that he wouldn't let her help on these items only made her feel even more undervalued and angry. She felt like Matt wanted her to just fade into the background. Didn't he know that she took a huge pay cut to be here? Was he threatened by her? Even her son, a college freshman, was making more money with his campus job.

Matt would give her some small special projects and from his view, he was giving her an opportunity to show her skills. But the way Rebecca saw it, it was just a way for Matt to get cheap slave labor on something that was unimportant. Plus, he obviously wasn't going to compensate her appropriately to complete more assignments.

Kitchen Table Talks:

Dad wasn't sure what to do with the situation between Matt and Rebecca. Matt was generally an easy-going, great manager. People loved to work with him and for him. Lately though, he knew there were things happening at home. Matt's mom had been diagnosed with dementia and experienced frequent falls down the stairs, so they were trying to take care of her at his house. Rebecca, on the other hand, had only been there a short time so Dad was forming his opinion based on what Matt was telling him.

Dad brought up the situation with Mom over dinner. Mom reminded him, "You have many resources." Then she asked him if he was the appropriate one to get involved or if HR was the one to deal with this situation. Knowing that Matt and Dad had grown very close through the years, she thought maybe Dad wasn't the most neutral party. He was great with people, but she lovingly reminded him, "Know your horse." If this was something beyond his expertise, Dad had other people in the company whose job it was to deal with personnel issues.

· · · · · ·

"We put constant pressure on ourselves to always be our best and then feel exhausted when we fail to live up to this unrealistic standard. And when we depend on our bosses for validation, the smallest bit of critical feedback starts to feel like a rejection of our entire selves." – Liz Fosslien

We've all been there, at one point or the other, where we felt overwhelmed at work. We're stressed, unappreciated, or treated unfairly. Maybe you try to keep it inside. You try to lock it up or suppress it a lot like that customer service representative who is trying their best to smile and hold in the anger because they've been taught that the customer is always right. But what about situations where a colleague takes credit for a job you did, or your boss is criticizing you harshly in front of everyone else?

If you've ever felt this way, you're not alone and there are ways that you can manage these emotions and several others, including anger, frustration, feeling unappreciated or bullied, and overwhelmed.

Don't Allow Your Job to be Your Reason for Living

Loving what you do is fulfilling. It's the best part of working because then it doesn't feel like work. Learn to practice a bit of detachment towards your job, especially when you do not work for yourself. Learn to understand that your job is not your whole life; it's a part of it, not all of it. Seeking validation from your job and your boss puts you in a possibly dangerous roller coaster of negative emotions.

Self-Awareness and Setting Boundaries

Emotional outbursts happen because we let them build and build until they just have to come out. Say you have a colleague who's always making innuendos, snide remarks or sarcastic comments about you at work to the amusement of others. To avoid an outburst that makes you look like the bad guy, put a stop to it in the beginning. Make it very clear that you don't appreciate such comments and report them to HR.

Learn to Compartmentalize

It is vital that you put your feelings into small little boxes. That is not about suppressing them. Our personal lives often have a way of seeping into our work life because you are one person who has many things happening to you. But it's important to do your best to keep them separate from work. Don't take your anger out on a colleague because you had a fight with your partner. If you can, before you get to work, take a few minutes on the ride or in the elevator and acknowledge those feelings - thank them for revealing themselves and put your feelings in the appropriate compartment. If what you are dealing with at home is too heavy and makes it impossible to concentrate at work, ask for a break to sort it out. You don't have to get into your personal details with your boss or HR in order for you to ask for time away.

Learn Your Triggers

We all have triggers that set us off or break us down. The way to deal with them is to recognize and avoid them. Say everyone is gathered in the break room talking about layoffs and cutbacks. If you know that you are a natural worrier, stay away from conversations like these. They will only increase your worry and ignite your stress, making you unable to concentrate on work. Also, recognizing your triggers helps you remain calm so that you can plan the appropriate reaction when they occur.

Clarify in Case It's a Misunderstanding

Before you burst into anger or take offence at a remark or situation, make sure it is what you think it is. Sometimes, it could be innocent and not intended to be offensive; sometimes, it could be a genuine mistake on the part of the other person. So, clarify, ask them what they mean or ask the other person why they said what they said. That will let you know how to deal with the situation.

Learn to say, "I apologize."

Sometimes, our feelings do get the better of us. When this happens and you say words in anger, apologize. Don't get defensive and don't play the part of the victim. Don't pretend like you didn't do it and hope the other person will just play along. Say you are sorry and calmly explain why you got angry or upset. Once you take responsibility, you will start to feel better. It also lets others (colleague and employer) know you value their relationship and not to put you in a similar situation in the future.

Talk to a Professional

Most organizations have in-house therapists or Employee Assistance Programs (EAP). Reach out to them. A professional has the tools and advice to help you deal with your issues. You should especially do this if the above listed suggestions are not working out. Sometimes, no matter how hard you try, emotions can leave you feeling overwhelmed and incapable. Don't feel scared about using your organization's resources. They are meant to be confidential.

To a large extent, managing your emotions at work is what sets you apart as a true professional. At work, that's the way you should be seen. Whether we want to or not, we have to deal with our negative emotions at work and the best way to do that is learning to manage them.

KITCHEN TABLE TALKS WITH DAD

Chapter 9
The Swain Hiring Method

"Sixty percent of all human communication is nonverbal body language; thirty percent is your tone, so that means ninety percent of what you're saying isn't coming out of your mouth."
~ Hitch

A new city statute forced Roy to raise wages. It would cut significantly into his bottom line, and he was upset that this was being forced upon him. As a business owner, he felt like the city was mandating something without caring or thinking about the effect on stores like his.

Four years later, Roy realized what a good thing the mandate turned out to be. When new hires came in, it wasn't just about being proficient to do the job. It was also about loyalty and that would only come with time. Every year since the statute, wages were mandated higher. In a lot of ways, the old adage, "You get what you pay for," played out here. He noticed more longevity and he noticed how it improved the culture within the company. The other thing he noticed about the culture was that the people who had been around a long time were the ones that upheld the culture. The new hires could either join in or be left out and most of them wanted to be part of the culture and the family because it was one of inclusion, allowing employee voice, exceptional customer service and rooted in excellence.

Roy had a huge sense of pride when he looked around at the employees in the grocery store. He saw people of many races, backgrounds and beliefs. Ultimately, the mission of the grocery store was to embody and exude love through the excellence that they were instilling amongst the employees. No one was more important than another. No customer was more important than another. The customer base was demographically very diverse as well.

No matter if you were an employee or customer, Roy wanted people to feel like they were valuable, as a valuable part of society. No one was seen as a thief just because they came from a certain place or dressed a certain way. Customers were not seen as just a transaction. They were greeted by name. These were the things that were essential to the culture in the grocery store that had given them such longevity in the community.

Kitchen Table Talks:

The day Roy found out that the mandate was official, he discussed the impact over dinner. The main question that came up was why the grocery store existed. Was it purely for profits? Over and over the answer was no. The store's mission had evolved through the years and was rooted and driven by a community focus to create jobs and give opportunities to people who lived in Chicago. The community had always needed jobs and it wasn't the government that would make the jobs, businesses would.

Mom said, "Do you know why our conversations move me so much? Because you and I have been talking and sharing for so many years, and I realized that our conversations are all about breaking generational curses. What we talk about impacts generations to come."

· · · · · ·

While there's a hierarchy in every company, it's always important that an employee is hired by the manager who will be overseeing them. There are formal parts to the hiring process such as the application and standard questions like why they're looking and what their availability is. Then there are informal parts such as if they look you in the eye, were they on time, and if you get the impression that they're looking to move forward in life.

Attire to interviews often matters. In the scenario of the grocery store, it didn't matter if someone came dressed in a t-shirt because that might be all they have or maybe they don't know any better because this is the first job they've ever applied for.

Once someone is past the interview and has been hired, it's not over. For the next 30 days, it's good to evaluate how they're doing. You want to assess if you were right in your impressions regarding their commitment, loyalty and desire to move forward in life. During this time, you will want to see how they take instruction, if they catch on quickly to new things, do they work independently, how often do they take breaks, do they come in late frequently or call in sick, are they good with customers, and if they contribute to the team.

Always look for those nonverbal cues as well. How do they respond? How do they move? What tone are they using in their voice? Lastly, always ask their boss what their thoughts are about the new hire.

Going forward, it's important to have regular performance reviews. While that is a more formal approach to giving feedback, it should not be isolated to that time. Feedback should be given much more frequently so that if there is any need for course correction, it can be done early on. Once you get to the formal evaluation, nothing on that written form should come as a surprise. If it is, you have not done your job in communicating with your employee.

Through the years, we've developed the Swain Hiring Method, which is focused on being a TRANSFORMATIONAL employee, regardless of your position. With that in mind, here are the important concepts that should be considered as you hire and continue to develop your employees.

Talent

This is commonly used to describe one's innate abilities typically in the following areas: cognitive, personality, learning, leadership, performance, motivation. Often the word talented is reserved for those who are considered high impact or high achievers. We believe that while there are those who seem to have a propensity to excel in certain areas and there are others who have the ability but may not currently possess the skills to do a task or job well. This doesn't mean they can't. They just haven't … yet.

Hire with the intention of developing people. A person may not look good on paper, but if "there's something about them" that fits your organization, be willing to bring them on.

Crucial to the success of your hiring is the following:

Relationship

What relationships do they talk about, what type of relationship could we have with them, and what type of relationships are they trying to have with their potential co-workers?

Adaptability

How quickly do they adjust to change? When was the last time they had to adapt suddenly? What was it and how did they respond?

Narrative

What parts of their story are interesting, even intriguing? Where do they come from? How do they want their narrative to change or evolve for the future?

Strengths

What are their perceived strengths and how do they see themselves using these strengths at work?

Focus

How focused are they on tasks in general and as it relates to the organization? Why do they feel they are or are not focused? This is important to us because there are often other things going on in their life that may distract them from certain goals. Developing a relationship with your employees helps them to feel your care and concern about their lives inside and outside of the work environment.

Outcomes

This is critical to any business. Sometimes you may hire people with a background that normally would preclude them from employment. Whomever you hire, employers must communicate to their employees that achieving outcomes (performance-based) is what keeps them employed. You may need to have hard and difficult conversations with employees but if you focus on outcomes, they will know exactly where you're coming from and what is expected.

References

Always check references. You'll learn about their personality, reputation, how they've been in relationships in previous work contexts, and what value they provided. Who you hire reflects who you are in the community and the values your organization believes in and hopes to embody.

Mission Driven

At the end of the day, it's about why your organization exists and whether an employee believes in that mission. To what extent are your employees embodying your company mission?

Ambition

Where do your employees see themselves long term? People often join an organization because they want a career in your industry or because they just need a job. If it is for the latter, don't stop there. Although this may be how they are introduced to you, every person has, and therefore has a right to achieve their dreams. It's your obligation to give them access to the resources they need to have those dreams manifest.

Teaming

This is a term by Harvard professor, Amy C. Edmundson. Teaming is teamwork on the fly. It is based on the premise that teams are not fixed over long periods of time. In high energy, fast-paced working environments, people have to be flexible and adaptable. For example, one day you could be on the register, another day you may be needed on the floor, particularly during certain times of the year such as

Christmas. Are you employees able to do this?

Intentionality

Everyone loves an underdog, right? Some people may feel like their back is against the wall, but they have the personality to give the job everything. They may be disadvantaged with certain situations in their life. Encourage your employees to live with intentionality from how they communicate with one another and other staff members to how they live their lives (goal-oriented and purposeful).

Organizational Culture

Designing a positive work culture needs to be a passion within organizations. The environment is critical to growth and development. Decide on your organizational culture. What does it embody? How would you want someone else to describe it? It could be family values such as patience, commitment to excellence (service to customers, knowledge about our products, developing as people), adaptability, and fun. Create a culture where employees know they're not alone, you believe in them and their future, and you are committed to assisting them in getting there.

Non-Verbal Communication

Non-verbal communication is such an important component of customer service and it's central to how often a customer thinks about returning to the business.

For example, the feeling a customer gets when someone greets them as they walk in or asks them if they need any assistance will keep that customer coming back. On the other hand, if a customer asks a team member for assistance and the response is an employee rolling their eyes or sighing in frustration, the customer feels like a bother or that they just interrupted your employee's agenda.

Affirmation

Many prospective and current employees have never felt that anyone was in their corner. They may have felt like no one cared and they've had to navigate life from a very defensive perspective. It's important to let them know that you recognize their value as a person and also as a member of your team. When you show that you're respecting them and encouraging them, they'll feel like you have their back. This affirmation is reciprocal. Don't affirm them so they can feel like they are indebted to you. Do it because everyone needs to feel humanized in a world that's often told them they're less than or unimportant.

Listening

Be slow to speak and quick to listen. The top-down model doesn't work. Employees are resistant to that model and the result is that you risk having high turnover, low morale, and more internal theft. If employees feel like you're operating like a dictator or treating them like robots, they become poor performers. When you listen to people, they feel heard and cared for -- they feel more connected, humanized, appreciated, and understood. Then they are more likely to be engaged and more focused on making a positive contribution to your organization and uphold the mission as well.

Chapter 10
The People Plan

"Success isn't about how much money you make;
it's about the difference you make in people's lives."
~ Michelle Obama

"SURPRISE!!"

A roomful of people cheered for Dad as he closed out his time at the grocery store.

Dad was fully retiring.

He had never meant for Roy to take over, but he now understood what a great thing it would be to pass this legacy down to his son. He was proud of what Roy had done and the ideas he had for making the store even more impactful in the community. For the last couple of years, even though Dad had already handed over the reins, they worked together, knowing that this day would come where the company would be fully Roy's and Dad would not continue to come into the office.

Roy had already implemented some new ideas. One was specifically about hiring past inmates. The grocery store was on the South Side of Chicago and his philosophy was that the store didn't exist only for profits. It existed to support and give back to the community and there was a new candidate to interview after Dad's retirement party.

The receptionist turned as she left the conference room, "Mr. Roy Davis will be with you in just a few minutes."

Diante took a deep breath. All his hopes were in this interview. He knew he would be a dedicated and loyal employee; he just needed someone else to believe it too.

He was grateful that the application to work at the grocery store hadn't gone back more than ten years in their question about incarceration. That meant that he could truthfully answer no to whether he had been convicted in the last decade. Luckily Diante's cousin's fiancée also worked at the store so she would potentially put in a good word for him because every last job he had applied to didn't hire ex-felons.

As he waited, Diante thought about the day that he went after his brother's killer. At that time, when he was 14, it was hard to watch this twenty-something year old man walking around, living his life while he desperately missed his 15-year-old brother every single day. He saw his grandmother hurting. Everyone in the neighborhood knew who the killer was. Even the police knew who it was, but nothing was being done. It was during gang violence while selling drugs that his brother had lost his life and Diante found the killer on the run before the police did.

Now, fifteen years and six months after being convicted of revenge murder, Diante sat waiting to find out the fate of this next phase of his life. If he didn't get hired this time, he didn't know what he'd do. Would he have to go back to the streets with the other inmates he knew? His time in prison had only added to his grandmother's hurt and he understood now that he hadn't solved anything with his crime. As a grown man, Diante regretted that young choice, but he couldn't change it.

When Roy joined Diante, he had already done a background check. He knew that Diante was still on parole. They shook hands and Roy asked some questions and eventually asked about Diante's record. Knowing that Diante was already 31 and hearing about the long length of time he had already spent in prison, Roy felt that this man had potential. It wasn't that the store searched out past inmates but being in the city meant that there would be opportunities to give some select people a second chance. Roy had already hired one felon in the past who had worked out, so he felt pretty comfortable with his decision.

"I'm going to give you a shot. I'm going to give you a chance."

Diante felt like God was looking down on him and presenting a huge blessing. This was going to be his first job ever and he was determined to show his appreciation by being the best floor stocking clerk the store ever employed.

As time passed, Diante continued to be loyal and dedicated. He was always on time and eventually, Roy saw that Diante's gift was in being a cashier. He was fast and it was through that job that Diante stopped being so stoic. At first, he approached being a cashier with his hands folded, lips tight and a guarded politeness. Soon the position broke his shell and he learned to smile and be personable with the customers.

Three years later, Roy promoted Diante to manager and handed him the keys to the store so he could open. He laughed thinking about the day that someone tried to steal a bag of popcorn and Diante had chased them down the street. But when Roy told Diante of the promotion, Diante declined the promotion, "I don't want to let you down."

But Roy wouldn't take no for an answer. Diante knew all the positions and knew what to do. He also interacted with the back office as well. After a bit of nudging, Diante accepted. He couldn't believe what had just happened and ran home like a little kid to tell his grandmother. She was going to be so proud.

For the next four years, every time Diante slid the key into the lock on the front door of the grocery store, it took him back to the day that he sat nervously waiting for his interview. The store now felt like family – it had saved him. He always wondered what would've happened to his life if he had not been given this chance and there was a big probability that he would've ended up on the streets in a gang. Instead, he was a manager with a family and a promising future. He felt like the people he worked with were like sisters and cousins. In fact, Diante acted more excited than Frank when he told everyone that he got a new place. Diante felt like an important person here. He had found his voice and been encouraged to use it. To him, the store embodied family, loyalty, honesty, strength and love and there was no place else he'd rather be every day.

Kitchen Table Talks:

Sharing about new hires over dinner was always exciting for Roy. His Dad had done the same thing for years too. Roy told Dad, Mom and Carolyn that he felt Diante had the maturity of someone who had spent significant time in prison. He wanted a fresh start with a new life without being in jeopardy of returning to prison. Diante clearly had a desire to go forward in his life, not backwards.

Not everyone who had a past had worked out at the store, but Roy knew that having a location on the South Side of Chicago meant that the community included those who had been incarcerated. This was his give-back to the community. It's like Mom had always said, "I'll help you get started and you can take it the rest of the way." He truly wanted to see these people succeed because part of the mission of the grocery store was to give everyone an opportunity. After that, it was the employee's responsibility to grab that chance.

In the upcoming days, Roy knew that Dad, Mom and Carolyn would come to meet Diante as they regularly visited the store. Dad looked at things a little more concretely and watched to see if employees were stealing time by coming in late or leaving early. Even if it didn't seem like a lot, it was an indication of their character and commitment to their job. Mom was the one who was always discerning. Sometimes she would quietly let Dad or Roy know, "Keep an eye on this one." Carolyn's background was as a business psychologist, so she was always interested in having conversations with people, finding out more about them and helping them to have a voice inside the company.

The next 30 days would tell Roy if he had made a good decision with Diante. The interview process never ended with just that short talk in the conference room. He would ask for feedback from Diante's direct manager and also seek out to hear the opinion of the other past prison inmates.

· · · · · ·

Creating a high EI company culture that leads to success only happens on purpose. It's just human nature to start to lean back when things seem to be running smoothly, but it's exactly at that time that your organization needs you to raise the bar.

It's not just about your organization, it's about the people inside your organization that make it all worth it. When there's an atmosphere that fosters communication, the best people rise easily to the top and teamwork, productivity and a general sense of company well-being happens. Even though everyone has a different job, everyone works together, respects each other's job and helps each other be their best.

The most important thing is keeping the lines of communication open. Share information freely up and down the chain and voice your feedback when it helps your organization. This way, everyone will be on the same page and understand what's going on, regardless of if they like a new idea or not.

Remember to always evaluate and measure what you've put into place. It's only in this way that you can improve your processes and company culture. And when it's time to celebrate milestones big or small, reward the people who helped you get there. No person's contribution is too small to be noticed. And with these times of recognition, you'll find more and more that your employees want to come to work not just to pay their bills, but also because they enjoy being a part of a company that values them.

Evaluating and growing your People Plan comes in stages:

Stage 1: Engage and Involve Your Employees
Stage 2: Review the Topic at Hand Concerning Your Employees
Stage 3: Review the Outcomes of the Topic at Hand Concerning Your Employees
Stage 4: Use your Data to Evaluate the Effectiveness of Current Policies and Practices
Stage 5: Map Policies and Practices against Outcomes
Stage 6: Enable Employees to Reflect on their Own Practices
Stage 7: Decide What Needs to be Started, Stopped, and

Kept
Stage 8: Clearly Delineate Roles and Responsibilities
Stage 9: Communicate Progress Regularly
Stage 10: Provide Sufficient Capacity and Resources

In business, it's the People Plan you put into place that dictates your success. Your organization is nothing without the people running it. Sure, they need to know how to do their job, but they need to know that their voice matters, that their ideas will be heard, and that they're making a true contribution to a collective mission they can get behind.

When you use the above stages as your guide, it lays out your organization in a transparent way. Everyone knows what that process looks like. There's an assessment phase that allows people to express their opinions about what they do and what they need. This creates buy in, and people will feel connected to it because they were a part of it. They feel like, "This is for us." Then once you get through the evaluation phase, there's a transformational phase where you ask what things will look like once it's over. And while this process is never really over since your organization will want to start back at stage one every time you complete stage ten, you'll have a transparent picture of what the vision is.

It's the leadership's job to inspire that shared vision. Oftentimes the why is the unspoken, important piece. When people understand the why behind why it matters, it helps you weed out the insignificant from the significant so you can concentrate on the important pieces. People need to understand why what you do matters and why where you're going matters because people don't always buy into what your organization does, rather they buy into the why behind it. Generally, that is why it connects to their values.

In conclusion, the way to achieve this level of high EI company culture, you have to be on purpose. That's the reason sharing concepts like EI, EV, IMPACT, IMAGES, M3C and the Swain Hiring Method with your employees is so critical to success. You don't want to skip any steps trying to get there faster.

KITCHEN TABLE TALKS WITH DAD

About Angela

Dreams are just dreams, but if you foster the right combination of inspiration, focus, and commitment, those dreams can finally become your reality.

Dr. Angela L. Swain's work is at an intersection between business, psychology, and spirituality. Spirituality is defined not by a particular religious ideology, rather how to live one's values. She has always had an underlying passion for discovering human mind abilities and for guiding others to tap into areas within themselves to foster empowerment and authenticity.

As a highly passionate, experienced, and professional Business Psychologist, Professor, Author, Consultant, and Leadership Development Coach, she has been a trusted advisor to innovative and highly motivated leaders and entrepreneurs. Her sole mission is to empower others to achieve their highest potential in business and within themselves.

Dr. Swain believes that we are all born with talents, skills, and unimaginable value that flow harmoniously together to make us unique. However, far too often, those very things that make each of us individualistic are buried away due to the hustle and bustle of life. The result is that our amazing potential goes untapped. Many find that the goals they set are not accomplished, or the balance in their life is not where they want it to be. This is where Dr. Swain steps in.

She will be your thought partner using an array of services, including:

→ Strategic Planning

→ Talent Management

→ Change Management

→ Succession Planning

→ Leadership Development

→ Diversity, Equity, and Inclusion

→ Anti-racism Initiatives

From personalized and group coaching, speaking, workshops, and seminars, individuals and organizations will be able to gain new insights and find out what makes them truly unique, their real selves. Once that is unearthed, they will find new opportunities they never knew existed to revolutionize themselves and their business to be even more impactful. These fully customizable services increase their self-mastery, identify what shifts they'd like to achieve, and help them reach new levels of success.

Dr. Swain holds a Ph.D. in Psychology from The Chicago School of Professional Psychology, a M.B.A from Saint Xavier University, a M.S.W. from the University of

Chicago, and M.Div. from Catholic Theological Union. She also holds a Professional Certified Coach (PCC) certification from the International Coaching Federation (ICF). This education, her own past struggles, combined with her desire to help others succeed, has shaped who she is today.

KITCHEN TABLE TALKS WITH DAD

KITCHEN TABLE TALKS WITH DAD

KITCHEN TABLE TALKS WITH DAD